FOCUS ON AL-ISLAM

A Series of Interviews with
Imam W. Deen Mohammed

in
Pittsburgh, Pennsylvania

ZAKAT PUBLICATIONS
Chicago, Illinois

Library of Congress Cataloging in Publication Data
Mohammed, W. Deen, 1933

FOCUS ON AL-ISLAM

Edited by Ayesha K. Mustafa
Typing by Bakerah K. Muhammad-Hafeez

Copyright 1988 by W. Deen Mohammed

All rights reserved. No part of this publication may be reproduced or transmitted in any form or by any means, electronic or mechanical, including photocopy, recording, or any information storage and retrieval system without the permission in writing from the author.

Library of Congress Catalog Card Number: 89-090728

Cover Design, layout, graphics
and Color Seperation by Atique Mahmood

Printed in the United States of America

INTRODUCTION

This publication represents a series of interviews conducted by Brother Robert Islam with his cohost, Imam Mustafa Hassain of the Muslim American Community of Pittsburgh, Pennsylvania. Through the years of 1983 through 1985 a total of six interviews have been selected from the appearances of Imam W. Deen Mohammed on their local television program, "Al-Islam in Focus." Those interviews are here presented in five parts.

It should also be noted that the spelling of Imam W. Deen Mohammed's name as it appears throughout the interview may differ from that as it is here in the introduction. This spelling in the introduction and henceforth represents a change to use that spelling that appears on the Imam's U.S.A. birth certificate.

ZAKAT PUBLICATIONS
December, 1988

A STATEMENT FROM W. DEEN MOHAMMED MUSLIM AMERICAN SPOKESMAN FOR HUMAN SALVATION

"I thank you, not as a Muslim, in the sense that the world sees Muslims, nor as a Christian or a Jew, or as a member of any religious denomination. We all have so much in common that is interchangeable and inter-related that I find it better to ignore religious labels and to deal only with a person's true beliefs.

"Therefore, I join with you as one who believes in an Almighty Creator of Heaven and Earth, for all of us have the right to speak and feel comfortable among people anywhere on earth. We are all of one creation and our belief in One Creator unites us in spite of artificial divisions of race, color and natural origin. We are united by the most powerful bond of all – our common human origin.

"The real issues that concern us and affect our social and economic destiny and the destiny of our children's children are vital to all and are more profound than any ideological differences that we may have.

"Our enemy is not the free world or the Communist world, nor Christianity, Judaism or any other religion. Our enemy is ignorance, racism, oppression, greed, and corruption. To eliminate these enemies, we must establish truth, justice, opportunity and compassion for all people. I have whole-hearted accepted this mission with the guidance of Allah. Please join me and unite to reconstruct our American lives."

PART I

May 1983

The life of our religion is defined in these terms: "A Community of people worshipping Allah." The family life is the first community. No family member should grow rich while his other members are poor and not try to encourage them or to bring them into some development or growth.

Imam W. Deen Mohammed

إن تعريف الحياة في ديننا الاسلامي هو بأن مجموعه من الناس مهمتها عبادة الله. وأول جماعة هي العائله. لايحق لاحد افراد العائله ان يكون غنياً والباقي فقراء وكذلك عليه ان يشجع إخوانه الفقراء على تطويرهم ونموهم.

ہماری مذہبی زندگی ان الفاظ میں بیان کی جا سکتی ہے ۔
ایک امت جو صرف اللہ کی عبادت کرتی ہے ۔ خاندان اس امت کا سب سے پہلا جزو ہے ۔ خاندان کے کسی فرد کو دولت مند بننے کا حق کیسے حاصل ہو سکتا ہے ۔ جبکہ دوسرے افراد خاندان محتاج اور غریب رہیں ۔ یہ کیسے ممکن ہے کہ متمول فرد اپنے اہل خانہ کی بہبود اور ترقی کے لئے کوشاں نہ ہو ۔

RI: As-Salaamu-Alaikum. Ladies and gentlemen we'd like to welcome you to our program "Islam in Focus" once again, and we have the royal privilege to have our leader, Imam W. Deen Muhammad with us today. We also have our co-host, Imam Mustafa Hassain here. And I'd like to give the greetings to both of the Imams – As-Salaamu-Alaikum.

WDM
    &   Wa-Alaikum As-Salaam.
IMH:

THE MUSLIMS: EMERGING AMERICAN LEADERSHIP

RI: We would like to begin our interview with Imam Muhammad. We were in Washington, DC about four weeks ago, and you were giving a lecture there. In the lecture you were saying that you were giving the views of the political situation of the African-American community today. And we know that you strongly approved of Chicago's first black Mayor, Mr. Harold Washington, and that you, yourself, may be running for office in an upcoming Presidential Election.

WDM: I thought that we had something special and something very unique to offer in terms of experience – a unique kind of experience we've had – and our growth as a minority people in this country, first as African-Americans and as Muslims. Most African-Americans have grown only as "Blacks" and not as Muslims. But we've grown as "Blacks," and we've grown as Muslims to work our way into the mainstream of Al-Islam. With the popularity of the Muslims in the world today because of the oil situation and I would say rebellious social disturbances in Iran, the Muslims have come forward and are in the eyes of the American people.

So, I feel that our country should take advantage of the opportunity to work with Muslims of the world who are agreeable with this kind of relationship. That they should work with those Muslim countries of the world, because Muslims belong to the free world.

Although I'm not saying that I agree with that terminology, but our religion promotes democratic processes. It sanctions and encourages the democratic processes. In fact, our religion is a democracy, and the Western world needs a relationship with the leaders of the free world. And we like to think of ourselves as the leaders of the free world.

There's a great Muslim population. There are the Muslims of Afghanistan. There are Muslims even in China. There's a sizeable minority of Muslims in Russia – not to mention the hundreds of millions of Muslims around the world in Africa, the Middle East, and the islands like Indonesia and the Philippine Islands. So, in my opinion, this history of ours as Muslims under the American circumstances has made us ready for effective rule and a new mind, and new sensitivities. I think our country shouldn't overlook this.

Maybe I'll never be President of the United States, but I don't think the country should overlook the fact that we have some unique kinds of mentality and personality and sensitivities in people here in America who used to be cut off from the American privileges, but now have grown with this country and have now become sensitive to the needs of American people – and we are also Muslims. To me, that's a powerful thing that America has going for it, especially in these present times.

African countries have become more visible during the latter half of the 50's, the 60's until now. The African countries are still becoming more visible. We're seeing the Muslim presence in them, because fifty percent or more of Africa is Muslim. Nigeria is mostly Muslims; the Sudan is Muslim. And we now need some kind of linkage between America and Africa, between America and the Middle East. This is what the State Department wants; this is what the President of the United States wants. Tell me, who could serve that better than me?

RI: Yes sir, we do have a unique position.

WDM: So I don't think we should overlook the advantages for America in having a man like me as President. The only worry should be is he moral? Is he a true man that all Americans can expect to be loyal to the Constitution of the United States and to the aspirations of the American people? Once they get past that hurdle, they should be happy with a man like me.

THE INFILTRATORS

RI: Brother Imam, that brings to mind a recent article on the infiltrators in the former Nation of Islam, now called American Muslim Mission, and the Hoover Plan. It would make you wonder if the people who had been supposedly representing America had been wronging or had misused the American people.

WDM: Well, there are some precious things about this American democracy. And we don't talk of civics in the way civics are taught in most American schools. We were taught civics to get by, just to meet with the requirements, and that was it. But since then I've studied American history, and I have come to really appreciate our concept of freedom. I think many Americans, Caucasians and others, misunderstand the concept of American freedom. I think that I'm with the Founding Fathers and the people who really and truly sense what this democracy is all about.

I see America as a country that challenges the individual and throws the individual into a situation where he is offered and enticed almost with the promise of freedom, the promise of enrichment. And at the same time it throws him into a situation where he has to be so competitive, that he also feels he's in the jungle. So it's a form of democracy that throws us into the conditions of jungle life, but at the same time holds out for us the hope of civilization, the hope of human dignity, and the hope of real freedom.

I think this is a great situation. I think that is why this country has made so much progress. If Americans lose sight on that idea of this democracy and that idea of freedom, I think we'll become less competitive in the world. And that is what's happening. We're becoming less competitive in the international world, because fewer American people, especially the leaders, are conceiving America in the way that it was conceived by the Founding Fathers and by the old pioneers of this country.

Now, if you were asking do I believe that such corruption can be? Yes Siree! There's going to always be some. That is also the blessed thing about America, in that even the criminal has a chance to move up if the good forces don't overcome him. Yes, they have infiltrated. And I believe that bad elements in our system and in our government, especially in the Intelligence Department, created a lot of those problems for us. Some of it was justified too, but much of it was not justified. I've met agents who had high regard and great respect for the moral principles of the Honorable Elijah Muhammad and for what he taught. They had high regard and great respect for his ability to bring about complete change from just idle life and vulgar life in individuals, to make them take on disciplined life and become industrious. I've heard them praise the Honorable Elijah Muhammad for those accomplishments and his Nation of Islam for those accomplishments.

So I know such persons in the Intelligence Department of the FBI and CIA. I don't think they would treat me unjust or have it in their heart to support some of the things that I've seen done that would not only break up the organization and destroy the power in the organization to keep it from becoming a threat to the safety or security of American society. But things have been done for many other reasons, for example just to discredit African-Americans and to weaken financial operations and financial establishment of African-Americans who happen to be Muslims. So these kinds of things that have been done against us, should never have been done this way. There's no justification for it at all. They say "Well, we feel that if you all keep those assets you can still be a threat; you can regroup." I don't believe that. The Caucasian man is an intelligent being, and those who have moved up in the Intelligence Department represent the better minds of the Caucasian people, when it comes to intelligence. But they have their psychologists, they have their people who know how to study situations.

I'm sure that they have as much sense as I have to know that the majority of the members of the Honorable Elijah Muhammad's movement were people who follow the Honorable Elijah Muhammad loyally. And the great majority of them were not people who were a threat to the security of this country. They were lawabiding people. Certainly, they believed the "White man was the devil," but they also believed that the "White" man was to be treated as a human being and to be treated with respect. They were told that they should obey the law of the land. They were religious people and their makeup was spiritual, just like the makeup of church people.

I'm sure that they knew that the Honorable Elijah Muhammad's teachings, in the way it was taught to his members, didn't encourage them to take up violence as a way of life. Their own Intelligence agents who were reporting on the Nation of Islam said they found them to be the most law-abiding people in America. So I believe that this is really deception on the part of the agency now – those who say "those Muslims are a threat and we have to make these moves." Hoover's move against the Nation of Islam was in part for the security of the American people. But in great part it was purely racist. And that is part of their old historical program in our country – to undermine minority people.

THE HOOVER PLAN PERPETUATED

RI: Is the Hoover Plan still being perpetuated?

WDM: From what we have observed, especially in Chicago, it seems to be certain substantial evidence that we have that indicates there is a core of people in the establishment or in the govrnment who have the intent of carrying out those desires against our community still.

RI: Would you say this has been done historically? This is something that's been going on ever since we've been in American?

WDM: Certainly. And I think it's something we have to look at and accept or at least face up to it. That African-Americans have always been worked against. Also there has always been some justification established for it, where they have organized and unified themselves, especially for business or economic development. Every time we've done that, we have been worked against. The FBI Department has knowledge that some of the Nation of Islam officials, some of the lieutenants, some of the captains, some of the ministers were engaging in unlawful activities – selling drugs. So we know of a minister, for at that time they were called ministers, who was convicted for some involvement in drug traffic and for accepting money from drug traffic into the donations or into the contributions of the temple. However, when you read the Hoover directives or counter intelligence directives for undermining and doing away with the old Nation of Islam or the Muslims of the Honorable Elijah Muhammad as a force or as an established entity to establish power, we see in his directives things that make us suspect them of being the ones who had brought about the moral deterioration. The Honorable Elijah Muhammad preached high morals and insisted upon high morals. He insisted upon his followers obeying the laws of the land. In fact, if any of his followers broke the laws of the land, he would ex-communicate them. If any of his followers were found guilty of violence or found guilty of breaking the laws of this land, of doing things that were low of a person doing the actions, the Honorable Elijah Muhammad would have them ex-communicated. That was the Honorable Elijah Muhammad's way.

ROLE MODELS FOR AMERICA

RI: That's right!

WDM: The Honorable Elijah Muhammad's teaching, as you know what he taught, of "the White man was the devil and the Black man was God," made us feel responsible for the "white man being a devil." He said, "the Black man *made* the White man a devil." He said, "a Black man named Yacub made the White man a race of devils." So we knew his psychology, which was a heavy psychology. It made us say "the White man is a devil, but we have to put up with him, for we made him that way." So he had a powerful psychology, and he wasn't worried about his people going out reacting.

I believe that the Intelligence Department infiltrated the movement with persons that would demoralize and contribute to the lowering of the moral life of staff members, of lieutenants, of captains, of ministers, so that the moral life would be weakened first. Because you have to weaken the moral life of people, before you can get them to do the wrong things. And I believe, whether it can be proven or not, that they, themselves, are responsible for a lot of that moral deterioration that came into the Nation of Islam during the late 60's and the early 70's. They are also responsible for the crime that was committed by the Muslims. I believe that was part of their program, to just weaken the organization and create an image of us that would justify their program to really unestablish African-Americans who were doing something to establish themselves financially and to get some dignity as poor people.

RI: Isn't that the goal or the role of corrupt leadership, to kill a movement upward and to try to kill them morally in the eyes of the people?

WDM: Yes. The thing that I want to bring out here is that I think we hurt ourselves and we really separate ourselves from a lot of good Americans when we point to this as a problem of the system. I don't think it's a problem of the system. I think it's a problem of bad elements in the system. And believe me, we have to become aggressive. African-American people now have to become just as aggressive in dignifying the masses of African-Americans economically and politically as you were in our efforts to dignify the citizenship with getting civil rights.

Now, the need is to form some kind of collective power, political power, an economic base for African-American people. And we need to do something to make our communities less dependent, our neighborhoods less dependent on the Federal Government, just as the Italian community or the Irish community has done. That's the big task for us – to bring up our communities where they will be no more dependent on federal assistance than the average American community. To do that we're going to have to become very, very aggressive.

What I am suggesting or indicating here is this. That we have been too complacent. We have been too tolerant. We haven't been aggressive. To be aggressive financially or aggressive economically, we have to have a plan for economic productivity. You have to have some vision of where you want to go financially or economically, of where you want to take the neighborhoods economically. You have to have some vision. Then you have to stick to that plan and not let political changes in the political atmosphere or changes in the cultural atmosphere, or do not let anything take you off your course. And to do that you're going to have to be willing to meet the challenge from rogues, thugs, hoodlums in the business world and bad elements in the government that will try to defeat your plan. I don't want to use terms that would make people think that I'm a violent radical or something, but it's wrong!

RI: That's right.

WDM: You have to accept that when you come into America, you have to be prepared for war - war with yourself, first. This is because your weak tendencies will be pulling on you and will be stopping you from progressing. But win that war against the bad elements in the country. And the best way to war against the bad elements in the country is to be morally right yourself, to encourage a healthy cultural environment in the neighborhoods, and go back to principles of high ideas of Christianity like the work ethic, if you're a Christian. Also, do the same thing in the context of your religion, if you're a Muslim.

We can't depend on the masses to do this — there has to be a select goup of people to do this. You need that select group of African-Americans to serve as a role model leader for the rest. And until we do that, then our people are not going to have the advantage that the Irish and the Italians have, because they have their own cultural institutions. They have their business institutions. They have their great leaders in business and their great leaders in their culture. They have their great leaders in politics. They have an organized sector to keep Irish and Italians in touch with their life. And until we get that, we're always going to be an inferior people when it comes to competing out here in the world economically, businesswise, etc.

Part of that is to fight the bad elements. We have to deal with them also. But I don't think we should have a crusade to wipe out sinners in this country, because that is American democracy too. You can be a free sinner in this country. But we have to contain ourselves and keep our own lives in order. We have to be prepared to do whatever is necessary within the law of the land to protect that.

THE AFRICAN-AMERICAN RESPONSIBILITY

RI: Actually, the elements that we see in our community today, with the prostitution, the drugs, and all the other ills that we find, the law department knows about this. They could stop it, if they really wanted to, couldn't they?

WDM: I don't know if they can stop it or not. I'll tell you what would help them put law enforcement in the position to stop a lot of this drug traffic. And that is for us to become more legitimately productive citizens of the country. You have the majority of

African-Americans punching clocks, in and out of jobs, on welfare and hardly owning anything of substance in their neigborhood or in the city. Our own neglect and our own shortcoming to make ourselves strong and productive is putting law enforcement in a bad situation. In many of our cities there is not a tax base anymore, as we know. In Gary they're crying, "Where's our tax base?" Well, Gary is filled with African-American folks. And they say the Caucasian business establishment has moved out or has deserted Gary. So we ask, are we equal to the White man?

RI: Yes.

WDM: Well then we have to develop a tax base there. And to get a tax base there where the Black citizens are, we're going to have to have businesses brought in there, and those businesses have to be bringing in money. That's the situation all over the United States where we are in great numbers. That's the situation in Los Angeles. That's the situation in New York. That's the situation in Chicago. But I really think out failure to be more self supporting, like Marcus Garvey taught or like the Honorable Elijah Muhammad taught, is responsible for a lot of the crime that we see in our communities and in our neighborhoods.

CONDITIONED BEHAVIOR

RI: The attitude that is in the minds of the African-American people, an attitude where we don't support each other, is a kind of peculiar attitude that we carry.

WDM: True. Robert, let me tell you something. This is not all our doing. Believe me, we are a people of equal ability, and we are a people who can really pull together and the truth of it is in the Cleveland Masjid. I went to the Cleveland Masjid, and we are building a structure there. Who was doing the work? It was the African-Americans of the community. They were there doing the work. And their spirit is good, and they're working like beavers. Now, if we can come together to do work like that without any white man, and if we can come together to put a mosque up and make it presentable and do excellent work, we can do anything we want to do.

So, this neglect on our part is not all our fault. It's conditioned behavior. And a lot of our so-called black leaders are responsible for it, because any time they come out here and tell us we need more jobs and fail to tell us that we need to shape up the family, then we have a problem. They get out here and tell us we need to get rid of Reagan, but they don't tell us that we need to get rid of our bad habits and the irresponsible way that we're living. We are contributing to the problem. Some people will say that our leaders are speaking as politicians; that's not their responsibility. I don't think another race could be in our situation and make such a silly reply. Our situation is so serious that a leader has to treat all of the serious ills.

THE NATURE OF THE DEVIL

RI: Okay. Is there a carefully thought out plan to destroy and corrupt the moral nature in the human being? Do we see this in the media?

WDM: Not by any visible means, but there is an invisible force. I think we have to identify this as the devil. And Muslims accept that there is a devil. In Christianity there's a concept of devil, and for Muslims there is a concept of devil. I think we have to accept that this is the devil; there is a devil war against the moral nature and moral life of the individual, so that the individual will be more susceptible to the designs and propositions of the devil. When your moral life is strong then you're not susceptible to the propositions of the devil.

So in identifying this, you can't charge it to any race in America; you can't charge it to any religion in America; you can't charge this to any business establishment in America. We have to charge this to the devil. How does the devil affect you? Through individuals that will carry out his business. So we have to look at society with that kind of knowledge and wisdom, and then what we have to do is make sure that we ourselves are not vulnerable. As I said, a select group of people have to be their brother's keeper. And there is a war on the ability of the human being. It didn't start just now — it's thousands of years old.

THE IMPORTANCE OF FAMILY LIFE

RI: Imam Muhammad, could you explain the importance of a stronger family life? How that family life, when it evolves, produces a good societal life?

WDM: In the Qur'an our Holy Book, social affections are highlighted to show that faith in God and social sensitivity are really the beginning of strength for a people. Social sensitivities by themselves don't make for a successful or victorious people. But once they have a principle stronger than their social life to protect the spirit and the tendencies in the social behavior then they have all that they needed. The life of our religion is defined in these terms: "A community of people worshipping God." Community is very important. God says in the Qur'an, "You are one community." And in another place it says in the Qur'an, "you are the best community raised up for the good of man." It means for all people, for the good of all people.

The family life is the first community. We're first born into the community of the family, and to show you the teachings in this regard from the Qur'an are consistent, it says, "Before God, family rights have a preference." And again it says, "Charity is for the near relatives and for the child of the road," meaning the person outdoors, and for the poor, and for the people who've suffered a tragedy. But then it says "first, for the near relatives, and to be spent in the path of God." But the near relatives are still mentioned.

Prophet Muhammad, peace be on him, encouraged Muslims to accept responsibility to grow strong families. No family member should grow rich while his other members are poor and not try to encourage them or to bring them into some development or some growth. Family life is very important for us as Muslims. But Christians will recall the early teachings and the old principles of Christianity, for it is very important for Christians, too. But this late life and all of these new fads and crazy lifestyles of ours have blinded us and have taken us away from the really human base and social base of life. And we need to come back to it.

INFLUENCES IN THE MEDIA

RI: We see that with the way things are projected with the media, it's the "do your own thing." It seems to appeal to the individual to separate the individual from the family, so one idividual is buying this and the other individual is buying that.

WDM: Let me tell you something, it will sound funny, but I was just listening to the radio one day and caught Bill Cosby. I like Bill Cosby and some other comedians. I decided to listen to him, and he got to one point of talking about his children. He said he didn't know why we just couldn't understand our children. He said we speak to them, but it seems like they can't hear us. "So we took him to the ear doctor, and the ear doctor says he hears good. Then we took him to a psychiatrist, and the psychiatrist says his mind is good. His ears are good, he is intelligent, he's healthy psychologically."

So at times the spirit and attitude of the people are unprotected. If you don't have clear direction in your life, or if you are not living in some kind of protective context, like the principles of faith or of a church or mosque, or a synagogue, or something like that; if you don't have a structure like that in which you are living and you're respecting, in time you'll become deaf to good advice. It is because the influences in society will just sweep you up into a gravity that you can't resist. And people will call you, and you can't hear. And they'll take you to the doctor and say, "What's wrong with his mind?" The doctor will say, "Oh, he's perfectly sane." At times this happens to society. And when that happens what you have to do then is appeal to the strongest appetite in the person. And the strongest appetite in the person is for individual survival. That's what society thinks.

So they will start appealing to the individual. "Do your own thing. What do you want? Get what you want." So they bring about individualism and a condition that's unhealthy for human society. Individualism is brought about. But it is just as a remedial step. We hope that once he becomes comfortable as an individual, that his sense would come back. Then he will join the human family again. He will join the "group life" and the group aspirations again. Now, I don't condemn this; I don't like it myself and I wouldn't do that. I wouldn't use such a strategy or such a psychology on people, but I believe the media is guilty of it. And I hope I get another chance to come on television. Maybe it is the only solution sometimes for many people. But I believe it is for a select group, and we have to keep that select group in touch with reality and out of those situations.

SELECT GROUP MODEL

RI: And that select group is a role model?

WDM: Yes sir. They should be the role model. And they have to be visible for the masses to see them and know what they're doing.

RI: But really, they are kept out of the eye of the public.

WDM: Yes, certainly. But I say it's our responsibility to let the masses know that there is a select group of people who have their life together and do have faith in this country and in themselves.

RI: Do we have to demand that right?

WDM: Yes, we do. We have to have that right.

COMMITTEE TO REMOVE ALL RACIAL IMAGES THAT ATTEMPT TO PORTRAY DIVINE (C.R.A.I.D.)

RI: Yes sir. Brother Imam, I know that we did have a committee called C.R.A.I.D. - a committee to remove all racial images that attempt to portray divine and speak to the psychological and the social effect, and as you explained in Dallas, the economical effect it can have on people.

WDM: Yes. What we offered was really something that we think is Christian as much as it is Muslim. I have studied the Bible, the Old Testament and New Testament, and I'm convinced that the Christian world is behind time. There is a program to advance and civilize human thinking in the neglected populations of the world, what they call savage, barbaric, illiterate communities of the world. The mission of Judaism and Christianity, and especially Christianity, is a mission of liberation, and the Bible gives a step by step program for achieving that.

I am convinced, and learned men in our religion and in Christianity, if they hear me will agree that the Christian world, the church is way behind times. It is an insult to human intelligence now. It is an insult to the intelligence of the masses that they would use these images that were designed to attract the attention of the savage, as a way of endearing people to God and to the Prophet Jesus, peace be unto him. We have to get rid of the imagery of religion.

RI: What you're saying is that we have to remove all images. We don't want to raise up another image and say that this is a "black man" who is god.

WDM: Any image is primitive. That's the habit of primitive man. That was the habit of barbaric man, to have an image of a human being as god. There are pictures of old barbaric rural societies confronting each other on the battle ground, and they would have the image of a human being on a pole or a stick. They would carry it into the war. They would carry the picture of a human being in effigy to strike terror into the enemy camp. So you would show him with a slit neck, his eyes popped out, a spear through his heart, and you would carry that effigy burning. That was a savage tactic.

And what we have in church life is something that was not introduced by Jesus and his disciples, but something that was brought in as a necessity or necessary condition. In fact, it was the priest who is called "Basil" who introduced the idea that Christianity should make a compromise with Paganism. And that what Paganism says in principle should be applied to Christianity, as to what Christianity says in principle. So what he was doing was reconciling principles in Paganism with Christian principles that were compatible. Along with that came all of the imagery of Apollo. As you know, Apollo was also called the Son of God – Son of Zeus, who was his father. The Roman people were always in the habit of presenting their gods in human figures or in human image. All of these deities of the Roman people or of the Greeks and even for the Western world and for Europe were represented in human forms. The same was done in Africa, and even in Egypt. Gods were given human forms.

So this was the old world of Pagan periods, a way of keeping the common man mystified, because they didn't think that the common man had the same intelligence as theirs. They believed that God had given talents to special creatures in the human family, and that they were the only ones that could be trusted with the future and with the welfare of their masses. They also believed that the masses had to be contained in fear or mystery. That idea was unacceptable in Christianity. And the plan in the Bible is to step by step graduate the intellect of the masses of the world, so that eventually the image would be removed. The New Testament says: "And Jesus took his disciples up into the mountain, and there they saw the configuration. And in that configuration was the light of Moses and the light of Elijah. The disciple said, but when they saw this they thought that Jesus was trying to say, 'Don't follow me anymore, . . . follow Elijah and Moses.' They say, but they saw the light come together as one light, and when they looked around for Jesus they couldn't see Jesus. Then they understood that he was saying that he came to fulfill the mission of the life of Moses and Elijah. So if he, himself, showed his disciples that kind of concept, then why should we show Jesus as a "White man with blue eyes and blond hair, or as a White man with brown eyes and black hair?" Why don't we show the people that Jesus should be seen in the content of his Message, in his Mission and his role, rather than in the flesh that suggests racism and racial superiority?

THE ESSENCE OF A LEADER IS IN HIS WORD

RI: The religious leadership today must still hold onto that concept.

WDM: That's the problem with the Black community, too. We have had great leaders, but we can't get past the physical image to really see the essence and believe in it. Wasn't Carter G. Woodson a great leader? Wasn't DuBois a great leader? So many of them were great leaders. Where are those men in our lives today? They're gone, because we saw them only as physical men. And successful nations of the world have had success, because they have had men who were able to get past the flesh to see the wisdom, the virtues, and the real qualities that represent the worth and essence of the person. They didn't attach themselves to the individual as such, but they attached themselves to his contribution to his legacy as a teacher, as a law driver, as a ruler, or as a businessman.

Dr. C. Eric Lincoln said in his book that the only institution that the Blacks have is the church. And because of the majority of

Blacks knowing only one institution, which is the church, then we are the most susceptible to this kind of physical attachment to leaders. We find that Blacks are more attached to Jesus as a person than Whites are. You can ask the average African-American, "Tell me something, what did Jesus teach? You just said to love Jesus." LOVE, LOVE, LOVE, but he taught more than that. He taught wisdom. And he represents principles and high ideals for bettering life. But we're in love with a person; we're in love with the flesh.

RELIEF VICARIOUSLY THROUGH THE IMAGE

RI: In Dallas, you said it was kind of a vicarious expression.

WDM: Certainly. A lot of psychology has to be used in order to understand all of these "peculiar" involvements we had. Certainly, suffering people can enjoy relief vicariously. Many of the slaves in our history suffered unbearable conditions. Although there were many slaves who were treated very well, we understand, but many of them had ignorant and very cruel slave masters. They would cry that one day this life would be over, and "I will meet Jesus." They would see Jesus with their eyes dead on the cross. He's dead, so you can't hurt him any more. "He's gone to the Father." So I believe that vicariously they enjoyed relief through Jesus crucified on the cross. Still, there is much more to say about that.

RI: When you have time, please do.

AFRICAN-AMERICANS MUST DEVELOP CULTURAL AND ECONOMICAL INSTITUTIONS

RI: I know we're developing programs for cultural and economical upliftment in our community. When we were in Philadelphia just a few weeks ago, you gave an address on how we're going to have to pull together our entertainers and our resources to begin to develop institutions ourselves.

WDM: Yes. One of our members in Chicago, a Muslim sister, allowed herself to get excited and behaved unMuslim-like. I hadn't seen this happen, since I have been in my southside neighborhood. And we have been living there for about 12 years. But some well-dressed, neat, clean-cut White Baptist missionaries came into our neighborhood and were ringing the doorbells at every door. They were on a mission to bring the people back to Christianity and back to Christian principles. So, this particular Muslim sister who belonged to our community told them she didn't know what they were doing in this neighborhood. She said, "You don't have anybody you know in your neighborhood that you think needs religion? Do you have any Blacks in your Baptist church?" They said, "Yes." She said, "Well, why didn't you send a Black in a Black neighborhood? We don't want you here."

I think she could have handled that situation in a way becoming to Muslims, but there is something in her to be admired. What I'm saying is this: We have needs that can only be taken care of, when we understand the total situation. As long as Blacks are not accepting to fulfill their obligation as preachers, or as religious teachers for we have churches, but a lot of our church leaders now are talking politics. A lot of them are talking "get the dollar," and they have left off the really fundamental and essential principles of the religion. As long as you have that then your community is irresponsible, nonproductive, and a threat to other communities.

So, we need a cultural movement. We need to get the cultural life of the Black Community back into our grip. In fact, we need to use our grip, for I don't think we ever have had a handle on it. We need to head it up. Not that we don't appreciate Bach or we don't appreciate the Beattles; maybe some of us do. Sure, I appreciate a lot of the Caucasian entertainers, and people like myself in our community also appreciate a lot of the talent in the Caucasians. We appreciate their dances; we appreciate their poetry, but we need an organized effort of our own. Other ethnic groups have it. We need a cultural institution that says it's a lasting thing and a lasting influence in the life of the Black African-American people. And I'm happy to say that the business effort has already brought about products to this end.

RI: Imam, I want to tell you, that I could drink from this water all day long.

WDM: It quenched my thirst.

RI: I'm quite sure that our viewing audience feels the same way that I do. That it is indeed a pleasure and a great honor to be with you and to have you spend the time with our programs which Imam

Hassain and myself are co-hosting, to be able to present Al-Islam and the views of our leader.

WDM: As a leader I would just like to express my appreciation on behalf of the community to you all for a very excellent program you have here. I hope that we will have more like this. Both of you seem to be very fine representatives for the African-American community and for the Muslim community.

RI: Thank you very much. Ladies and gentlemen, you know I'm very seldom at a loss for words. But today I'm at a loss for words now, because we've had a very informative two hours with Imam W. Deen Muhammad, the Muslim American leader. My co-host, Imam Hassain has let me carry the whole ball, and I thank him. Our Imam Hassain is the kind of man who always pushes his youth forward; he pushes us forward to do more. I would like to state that this is our program, "Al-Islam in Focus." We've had the privilege to have our Leader, Imam W. Deen Muhammad with us. We hope that you've enjoyed our program and that you'll tune in and watch us again. Thank you! I give you the greetings from all the prophets from Abraham to Muhammad, the greetings of peace in the Qur'an and Arabic language — As-Salaamu-Alaikum.

IMH: Wa-Alaikum As-Salaam.

PART II

September 1983

Muslims can't accept to live in the world and see other people develop in businesses and they just be employed waiting for other people to create an opening for them. Allah says: "Seek the Hereafter with all the means I've given you, but don't neglect your share of responsibility in the physical world."

Imam W. Deen Mohammed

يجب على المسلمين ان لا ينتظروا من الناس أن يوجد وا لهم العمل فإن الله امرهم بان يستخدموا كل الوسائل بحلال لكي يتحملوا مسؤلياتهم بالدنيا.

RI: As-Salaamu-Alaikum. Ladies and gentlemen, we're glad to be in your homes. We have the privilege to have our Leader, Imam W. Deen Muhammad here with us once again, and we would like to warmly welcome him. As-Salaamu-Alaikum.

WDM: Wa-Alaikum-Assalaam.

RI: We also have our co-host Imam Mustafa Hassain with us again, and we'd like to greet you. As-Salaamu-Alaikum, Brother Imam.

IMH: Wa-Alaikum-Assalaam.

RI: We would like to let the Imam know that we feel it a privilege and a great honor to have you here, for we know you have a very busy schedule. At your last interview in the Pittsburgh area we had a lot of very favorable comments on the subjects we spoke on and your answers. But first, ladies and gentlemen, I would like to read from the introduction of Imam Muhammad's last book just written, entitled *Religion on the Line*. It says:

> "Imam W. Deen Muhammad was born to the Honorable Elijah Muhammad (Leader of the Nation of Islam 1934-1975, and one of the leading figures in the African-American struggle to achieve dignity and respect in America) and Sister Clara Muhammad on the 30th day of October 1933 in Detroit, Michigan.
>
> "Imam Muhammad has received the Walter Reuther Humanitarian Award, The Four Freedoms Award (among whose past recipients have been President John F. Kennedy, Mrs. Eleanor Roosevelt, and Dr. Ralph Bunche), and a multitude of proclamations from mayors and government officials.
>
> "He has lectured at Malcom X University, Duke University, Howard University, and the University of Maryland Law

School, Wayne County Community College, and numerous other colleges and auditoriums nationwide and abroad.

"He has headed interfaith "Jubilees" in scores of major cities and has been a keynote speaker at the American Academy of Religion, the World Council of Churches, and the Jewish community. He also has a weekly question and answer column in the "American Muslim Journal" (Now known as the Muslim Journal) and has written several books. He also has a weekly radio program that is heard nationwide.

"Imam Muhammad has traveled extensively to the Middle East, China, and the Carribean Islands, and has been the personal guest of Egyptian President Anwar Sadat, Prime Minister Forbes Burnham of Guyana, and King Khalid of Saudi Arabia. Also, Sheikh Sheguru of Nigeria and President Zia Ul-Haq of Pakistan had audience with him here in the U.S.A.

"In an unprecedented move, the Tenth Annual Islamic Conference of Ministers of Foreign Affairs (meeting in Fez, Morocco) invited but one American to observe this historic and critical meeting — Imam W. Deen Muhammad. This choice heralds a growing appreciation for the strength of the Islamic movement in America under his dignified and effective leadership.

"Imam Muhammad's keen scriptural knowledge of the Qur'an and the Bible and of human nature has enabled him to direct attention to the need of strong moral leadership necessary in establishing true human dignity and human rights. His efforts to revive commitment to proper patriotism in America, and support the desire for peace, human dignity and family unity has won him many humanitarian awards, citations and proclamations, and his name and works have been entered into the Congressional Record."

MUHAMMAD THE UNIVERSAL PROPHET

RI: We would like to begin this conversation with Imam Muhammad by asking him a question: What was the mission of the prophets and specifically Prophet Muhammad?

WDM: The theme in scripture, that is for the Bible and Qur'an, is the liberation of humanity. This liberation in religion as we understand it is mainly a liberation of the conscience of man. The Qur'an and Bible have the same theme. And Muhammad the Prophet, peace be upon him, the last of God's prophets, peace be upon them, was as we believe the Seal of the prophets. That is, he is the Universal Prophet. Other prophets we believe addressed human life on a regional dimension, whereas Prophet Muhammad addressed the needs in human life on a global plane in a global dimension.

JESUS - A SIGN OF PROPHET MUHAMMAD

RI: We say that Prophet Muhammad is the Seal of the Prophets, and I think in the Holy Qur'an it says that Jesus was a sign pointing to Prophet Muhammad. What do you say regarding this?

WDM: It does say that, and we accept that. The Qur'an does say that Jesus was the Word from his Lord. And this is in agreement with what the Bible says of Jesus. We understand that a word means a sign; that Jesus himself was a sign. After all, when we look at a word, until we study that word, what is it but a sign? It holds a meaning, but we have to study the word in order to get the full meaning of that word.

Jesus was a sign of what God intended for man — the good life that God intended for man, and how that good life has to struggle and even be abused and rejected. It has to rise and fall. But eventually God establishes it in His own good time. Jesus is also a sign of that which would come in the end of the world. And we do believe that Prophet Muhammad fulfilled that major sign that Jesus pointed to for the future of the world.

RELIGION SHOULD EDUCATE SOCIETY

RI: Yes sir, Brother Imam. It says in the Bible that Jesus said, "Blessed be the poor" in his Sermon on the Mount. And Prophet

Muhammad said, "My community began with the poor and shall end with the poor." Then, you say that the focus in religion is to educate the masses?

WDM: Certainly it is, with no doubt! I believe most of the learned men in Judaism, Christianity and our religion would agree that the major focus in religion is on the need to educate society — fallen society. And there is the need to stimulate an interest in the upper class or in the leadership to keep alive the faculties that are in the masses of the people. As civilization grows, demands will get heavier on us. As demands get heavier on us, then we will need more from the common people.

What the scripture does is to very delicately treat this problem. Instead of denouncing the leaderships of the world as traitors, as people who would betray this common interest, in most of its addresses it is saying to the leaders "to be aware of your needs." That if they hold back the potential in the common people, eventually their own needs are going to be deprived. They will not have what they need, because leaders have to depend upon the masses. On the other hand, the more civilization progresses, the more complex life gets. The more inventions come out, and the more is demanded of man that he functions on a higher or broader level, that he is able to do more.

If man is not able to do more, what can we do in this modern day with millions and millions of people who do not have any education? Without education, they are nothing but a burden on the world in this modern day. We don't need man to do the work of beasts; we don't need man to do the simple task anymore. They have machines; they have many things that can take care of that. We need man to have a higher functioning ability. Society should not ignore that need in humanity to educate humanity and give humanity what it needs. As much as man shows that he has the ability to learn and fulfill his own capacity, then society should provide for that. We do not condemn industry or any sector of society for their shortcomings as much as we condemn ourselves as religious leaders, because we're supposed to be in touch with God's Word. And it is God's Word that has advanced this theme.

THE RESPONSIBILITY OF RELIGIOUS LEADERSHIP

RI: Regarding religious leadership, is this a responsibility that God has placed upon it, to bring the Word of God and the better understanding of human life and human values to humanity?

WDM: Yes The responsibility is even more on the religious people. If we say we are the Ministers, the Imams, the Rabbis, or any people who say they represent the Word of God, then if we're true to that we will accept the responsibility to keep the God-conscience of society alive. That's our responsibility more than it is anybody else's responsibility.

RI: Why would these leaders want to hide or keep the knowledge away from the masses of people? Is it to stay in some kind of position?

WDM: I think ignorance is their main problem and the biggest problem. We make the wrong decisions. We fear too much, and the biggest problem is trust. You have to trust God's creatures. If Allah God has put into His people the ability to live on a noble plane — and that is what we believe in religion — that He created Adam on a noble plane, and revelation came behind Adam to restore man to the noble plane that God intended for him in creating Adam. This is what we believe. So if we don't have faith in the ability of people to manage the ordinary burden of life, then we will oppress people. We will suppress that potential in them. We will make mistakes. And I believe that man makes more mistakes than he commits sins; although he commits too many sins also.

RI: But you are saying the majority of things that you feel we do wrong are things done out of mistakes?

WDM: I believe it is by mistake, yes sir.

THE DARK AGE

RI: Imam Muhammad, I know you've heard a lot about the role of women in Al-Islam from the time of Prophet Muhammad to the present role of the woman in the American Muslim Community.

WDM: It is interesting that Prophet Muhammad, peace be upon

him, didn't just go right to the social ills and begin condemning or setting up laws. He did not say, "This is finished! Do this no more!" That was not how it was done. Prophet Muhammad was born in Mecca. And Mecca in the time of Prophet Muhammad, perhaps, was the darkest spot in the "Dark Age" or the period of Jahaliya. And Jahaliya translated literally means ignorance. In that period of ignorance on the Peninsula of Arabia, where Mecca is located, where the holy precincts are for Muslims, there was the worst degree of ignorance and the worst degree of immorality. And it was Prophet Muhammad who addressed it in a very tactful way; he was very tactful! Allah inspired him and gave him the direction. Alcohol was not stopped immediately. Slavery was not abolished immediately. But his program was a program of broad gradualism.

Now you mentioned women. The liberation of women was the same program, a program of gradualism. But it was gradualism that had in it such strong principles that reached the conscience of man, that reached his heart as well as his intellect. Therefore, it is impossible for a man to call himself a Muslim and continue to practice those things that were wrong.

RI: It is very interesting. And when man's vision is broadened, can he stay in the same narrow path?

WDM: No, he can't, not if he's going to be of the religion of Al-Islam which has the spirit of morality, the spirit of devotion to God, love for the Prophet and love for one's fellow man. These are so strong, that it's almost impossible for a man to be in touch with that kind of a religion and continue to commit big sins against society.

AL-ISLAM DEVELOPS FAMILY LIFE

RI: Brother Imam, there is another question I'd like to ask you. Our responsibility as Muslims is to reach as many people as possible with the message of Al-Islam. Do you feel that it is the African-American people who are in a greater need of Al-Islam, because of our situation and our history?

WDM: Our social researchers tell us that the Black family or African-American family during slavery was destroyed. Also, I don't think there's another religion in America that requires as much attention to family needs, or ask that we give as much attention to family needs as this religion. Personally, I don't want to present myself as one selling his religion on the program. But yet I believe that this religion just happens to be perfectly designed to treat the ills of the underprivileged, deprived African-American people. The experiences we had in slavery did away with that family cohesiveness. Now since slavery we were free to restore the family unit. Some southern families were very strong. So many of us did regain a strong sense of family after freedom. We don't know exactly what the condition was immediately before slavery, but we do know that during the time of slavery and in early history there were many Africans who had high civilizations that were equal or surpassing what we see in the world today, when it comes to human sensitivities and civilized behavior. And although we did come to some kind of strong sense of family after slavery, we still can see the need to develop what is the social concept of the family.

I don't think it's good enough yet. We're still responding to desperate needs. So the mother will say, "Son, I don't want you to lay around the house here and not get an education. You have to accept your responsibility as a man in the future, and I'm not going to let you sit around here and stay uneducated." So if you wanted to play hookey and mama caught you, you were in trouble. That was the southern woman and the southern mother. A lot of our northern mothers were like that, too, because they came from the south or their mothers came from the south. And if you were caught laying around the house and not doing any work when I was a young man, you would hear about it.

Once my father told me, "Look, you say you did your chores?" And I said, "Yes sir." He said, "Well, it's early in the day and people are working. You are not in school now, so go to work. If you can't find anything to do, Wallace, go out and check around the house. If you find leaves on the trees and none fell, just count those on the tree. Just do something. You had better be busy at someting!" Well, that stuck with me, and I never forgot that. It's important to keep your life functioning. It's important to use whatever God has given you, because everything operates just like our muscles. If you don't use them, they will collapse.

So I can understand that and appreciate that kind of teaching from our parents. However, I do believe that we need to improve our own knowledge of the family and family needs and see that in a social context. You shouldn't marry just to marry or just to have a beautiful woman or a beautiful husband. You should not marry for reasons like that. The business angle is a strong one also, but you should not marry just to improve your financial situation. The greatest thing to marry for is to preserve your social life, so that the meaning of man and woman stays in place.

We need parents who will be responsible for giving young children what they need in order to establish themselves as adults in the world. Improvement has come about in the whole society to raise the level of man's life because of good strong families. So we need to see the role of family in advancing human society as a social role. And we need to understand that this first unit is still the basis of society. You will find weak families when you see husbands and wives who are together for reasons other than to establish their children in the world and to see their life through their children advanced and making a contribution to the whole of society. When that is lost, then you can expect that those people are not very strong in their society.

RI: That is beauriful. I can see how a man's and a woman's life can travel through their children. And is this the essence of their life?

WDM: It has to be. All of us want to meet our God, when He calls us. We want to be accepted by our God. But what about the future, if I don't have a concern or an interest in my children's future? Isn't that my life? Where did my son get his flesh? Didn't he get his flesh from my wife and me?

RI: That is right.

WDM: So, that's my flesh. If I don't have an interest in my son, who is a new and tender life growing in our flesh, then what right do I have to go into heaven?

FAMILY RIGHTS HAVE A PRIORITY

RI: Yes sir. So what you are saying is that the responsibility of the family is a development of society?

WDM: Certainly it is! You cannot separate the two. That is why in this religion family is a major concern. Allah says that before God family rights have a priority. Let me repeat this: family rights have a priority before God. I'm obligated to see that my family has the basic needs, before I'm obligated to go and see that somebody else has those basic needs. I'm obligated to be charitable to my own children, to my wife, to my grandmother, and the needy in my family, before I'm obligated to see that for a stranger or a distant people or for this project to be funded. Charity starts at home and spreads abroad. This is Islamic also.

FAITH IN ALLAH, OUR FOUNDATION

RI: Regarding the economic situation that we see in the world today, as a people do we have a foundation or are we still in the process of building a foundation as an economic group?

WDM: That is in regards to the Muslim membership?

RI: Yes sir.

WDM: Yes, we have a foundation, and we're in the process of strengthening and enlarging that foundation. The first foundation is gratefulness or gratitude. To be thankful to Whoever made what we enjoy possible. And the most miserable person on this earth is enjoying something. If they weren't, they wouldn't be here anymore. So the first foundation is to have a healthy appreciation for whatever we have, no matter how small it is. To be thankful to God is the first foundation. We call that Faith or Taqwah, the love of God or faith in God. And from that foundation God obligates us to establish ourselves in the world, because He created us to live in the world. We do not live outside the world; we have to live in the world.

So Muslims are obligated to establish academic foundations – institutions of learning. We can't accept that an un-Islamic society provides all this for us. We have to be ourselves involved in providing these things, either with other people or independently. If there's enough of us we should do something independently as a demonstration of what Muslims can do or what Muslims are obligated to do. So we have to have an academic foundation. We have to have some business. Muslims can't accept to live in the world and see other people develop in businesses and they just be employed, waiting for other people to create an opening for them. No, we cannot accept that, not if we accept our religion. God says: "Seek the Hereafter with all the means I've given you, but don't neglect your share of responsibility in the physical world." This is our religion. And we are in the process of strengthening the foundation and also extending and enlarging the foundation. We will not be satisfied, until we live a complete life and make a complete contribution to society. That means we even have to be involved in the political processes.

RI: That's the next question I really wanted to ask you, especially with the political situation and the political climate in the world today. Can the Muslims have an impact on society and the political arena?

WDM: Yes, we can. We're obligated to do that. We're obligated to share responsibility with the rest of the members of society. And that includes the political responsibility of government.

ISLAMIC CONCERNS FOR HUMAN RIGHTS

RI: Imam Muhammad, on the international level, in the small and developing countries, and in Islamic nations, do you see a growing concern for human rights or for humanity?

WDM: There definitely is. In fact, there has always been a strong concern in Muslim circles for human rights. But the spirit of the religion rises and falls for us just like it does for Christians or for any other society. Prophet Muhammad brought this to our attention, peace be upon him, when he said that his nation would go to sleep. He said that the thing that would cause his nation to go to sleep would be the love of the material things of the world. Now if we study the history of the Islamic world since the Prophet, peace be upon him, and his Companions - those heroes in the early years in the development of the Muslim life and community, you'll see that when they were eagerly seeking to serve the good of not only a

Muslim life but the good of a common man's life, there was progress.

Now when their interests went from that to material things, to building up empires of wealth, then the light went out and the Islamic community of this world went down and lost its place in the lead of the movement to liberate and educate. They lost their lead in bringing on what we call the "Renaissance." And the Renaissance movement was then taken over by the Europeans and by the West. Ever since then the Islamic community has been somewhat in the background. Now we realize that, and we are trying to come out front again. But to come out front, we have to go back to the number one concern, and that is appreciation for what Allah has given us and to share that with humanity.

RI: That brings about another question that is on my mind. The role of the prophets in our individual lives, for Allah reveals His Words to the prophet as exemplified in the life that the prophets lived. Then do we as individuals live or go through those same situations in our individual lives?

THE REAWAKING OF THE ISLAMIC MIND

WDM: Yes. We are all the same. We are all one essence. And in time we all experience the same thing – in time. Maybe I'll never experience what my ancestor a thousand years ago experienced in totality, but I'm experiencing some of what my ancestors a thousand years ago experienced. We do have similar experiences. And Prophet Muhammad is a universal model. So whatever we experience in our life, we can find a likeness of it in the life of Prophet Muhammad. And if we find ourselves faced with great difficulty, we should turn not only to the Word of God in Qur'an, but we should also turn to the Seerah — the history, the symbol of the prophet, and see if he met a similar situation. That is why he's called the example. See if he faced a similar situation, and then see how he handled it.

I think that is what the learned of the Islamic world are doing now in Saudi Arabia. They had a big conference there recently on human rights and the need for more things to be done. They established a survey. So we are conscious of what the human dignity is, and we are trying to respect that. Our religion requires that we respect that, but we could do more. Now we are happy to say that in Saudi Arabia, if anyone needs an education and I don't care who he is – even the foreigner, he can get it there. The Government provides education on all levels for everybody living in Saudi Arabia. Much is done to help Third World people by Saudi Arabia also, so that other than the Saudi's will be able to get a good education. Perhaps we don't know that Saudi Arabia is the biggest contributor to UNICEF. UNICEF, as you know, is formed mainly by the United Nations and mainly of Western support. And it has done miraculous things as far as aiding the needs of common people and the Third World suffering nations and suffering parts of the world. Saudi Arabia, perhaps, is the biggest contributor. Relatively given the size of Saudi Arabia, it gives much more than its share.

RI: And that takes us back to what you originally said about the Muslim countries are now taking themselves away from just material gains for themselves.

WDM: Yes, that's changing. With the resurgence of Islamic conscience in the world that we see sometimes in a way that does not represent exactly what's happening – we see it only as a political image. With this resurgence we are seeing an awakening of the conscience of the Islamic man, the Islamic person to serve the best needs in the society, to come to the aid of the deprived person. We are seeing that, and I think that on the whole we are doing a good job. Although there is a lot of room for improvement.

AL-ISLAM – A PRACTICAL RELIGION

RI: That Islamic conscience that's in a man – when it begins to be revived, it runs so very deep! I guess it moves him to do things that seem to be almost impossible.

WDM: Well, no. I don't think so. At times I think I have been naive, and I think I have tackled the impossible in my growing up. But I don't think the religion is that way. I think the religion is a practical religion, and the emphasis in the religion is on what is practical – on faith and what is practical. I think that most of the Muslims are not trying to perform miracles; they're only trying to do what is decent of them and what is practical. And we can do that.

RI: Well, that's almost a miracle in this day and time.

WDM: Believe me, I understand that. But if you keep your mind in the context of your own life and keep your mind in the framework of your own life, then it is not so difficult. But if we live outside of the framework or the context of our own life in America, it's like a bodiless being and that being has no protection. So it would be terrible.

What I mean by that is this country offers us the freedom to choose our way of life. America is perhaps a place where the idea of freedom is developed to its highest degree. It even carries freedom beyond the definition of freedom that's held by civilized man. It stretches the meaning of freedom so that it even accommodates the uncivilized man. So in this kind of environment, if you don't live within the context of your own religion or in the context of your own life that you have chosen, then you're going to get swept away; you're going to be tossed about in the winds.

RI: That which you just said, in that it even stretches beyond the concepts of what the civilized man understands freedom to be. Is that good or bad?

WDM: It's good and bad. In America it's good, because America has established that this country is a country where a person can come and can live their life and do whatever they want as long as they respect the laws of the land. So you don't have to be a Christian to come and live in America. You don't have to be a God-fearing person either; you can be an atheist, and you're welcomed. No one can say, "You have no right to live in America, because you're an atheist." No one can say, "This man is not a morally conscience person; all he wants is money." You can't put any person out of America because he wants money, or because he wants money number one with nothing else coming first. He's free to grow in America.

His influence is going to grow eventually, if he's allowed to progress. Eventually his influence is going to reach me. Now when his influence reaches me, perhaps he's selling things to me, he's appealing to sentiments in me with his commericals that push his products that are unhealthy for me in the context of life that I have chosen. Now, if I don't know that context, if I'm not in that context, then the context of my life is subject to be destroyed by the influences of that man. But he has that right. I can't deny him that right, not in the nation we call America. This nation provides for that. And I think it's pretty good.

RI: I can appreciate what you're saying. But doesn't that cause a lot of destruction?

WDM: Maybe not as much as would happen if one 'holy-holy' becomes the dictator for all America. We might have more destruction.

JIHAD MEANS TO STRUGGLE

RI: There's term in Al-Islam that is called "Jihad." Would you explain. I think many of us when we hear the term "Jihad," we think it's just of holy war. I think that's the common understanding.

WDM: Certainly, because it has been used to identify with war more than anything else. But if you read the Qur'an you don't get that meaning, because God says "Jaheedu" from the word jihad as a verb. The verb is Jah-eedu when we're addressing many — the plural. God says "jaheedu." And He said, "Fis sabillaah," or in the way of God with your persons, your wealth, etc.

What is the purpose of jihad? The purpose is to improve society, even if in the war. If people will war against us or will aggress upon us to take away this precious life, then we have to also 'jihad' in the battlefield. We have to struggle in the battlefield, too. But the word jaheedu is very conclusive. It means struggle in everything that God has established for you to do. There's a need to exert yourself at times, and if you're not prepared to exert yourself, you will lose your moral life; you will lose your intelligence. You will lose everything, because there are temptations and influences that will induce in us tendencies to give up on life, period. So if we are not prepared to jaheedu — to struggle — to persist — to exert ourselves to put forth effort, then you will lose all that.

The emphasis on jihad in the Qur'an and in the life of Prophet Muhammad was not for the purpose of conquering lands or overthrowing nations, it was for the purpose of liberating the higher instincts, the higher aspirations in man. And we are to put forth this effort for education, for cultural development, for business, for government – for everything. If people will try to suppress that or dominate you and deprive you of that, you should be even prepared to struggle with your physical life, to put your life on the line and fight if you have to. But we live in America; we don't live under Islamic law. So in this country we trust that this country will remain civilized and protect the rights of Muslims, as it protects the rights of its other minorities.

THE MEANING OF HAJJ

RI: Sir, the other question that I wanted to ask you is about Hajj as a symbol. What does Hajj really represent in the life of mankind?

WDM: The highlight of Hajj is really the coming together on Mount Arafat. And it is said that Prophet Muhammad has said, Peace be upon him, that the one who misses Arafat has missed his Hajj. So Arafat is very important for Hajj. Without Arafat, there is no Hajj. And Allah says in the Qur'an that He has made us into tribes and families, which means smaller units of man and bigger units of man – tribes and nations or tribes and races. He made us this way, not that we should stand over each other, but that we should get to know one another and become acquainted with each other. This expression in the Qur'an is very rich. It's a profound statement. It is *very* rich.

If you study the word "taawrafu," you will find it means "getting acquainted, meeting each other, or to know each other." This is done by sharing information with each other. So how would the modern world have discovered what we call now mortal weapons, gunpowder, or even the rocket, if someone had not gone from the West to China and found them using black powder, later called gunpowder? So how would they have found that, if they hadn't gone and met the Chinese? God did not deposit everything in all people. He only deposited the potential in everybody, but He put the opportunity in many places of the world for that potential to come forth.

The environment that we find in Africa is an opportunity for that potential to come out. But that enrivonment in Africa does not give us everything. The environment in Europe will give us something different from the environment of China. In the Philippines it is different from being in America. Allah wants us to come together, although it was He Who spread us out. But we find these rich environments, and He wants us to come together and share what we have found with each other to make one big strong, great, and progressive world. That's the main purpose of the Hajj. It is to bring Muslims from different nations and different nationalities and different lands to come together and share with each other their knowledge, so that all of us would have broader knowledge of what the global community offers man when they work together.

RI: So you are saying that when we do come to Hajj, we come as one humanity?

WDM: Yes. We can't come any other way, God says that you should get to know each other, not stand over each other and not to despise each other. Prophet Muhammad, in his last sermon said and appealed to his people from the depths of his heart. And he would call on Allah, God Almighty, occasionally to have as his witness. He said, "God, be a Witness that I have delivered the Message." And in this major sermon of Prophet Muhammad, he said, "There is no superiority of a white over black or black over white. There is no superiority of a national or of an Arab over a non-Arab. The only criteria in this religion is your good deeds — Taqwa — faith in God and in good deeds." It is your behaviour in God's eyes which will be the criteria.

RI: Then the goodness that we express is the key for humanity?

WDM: I believe these same teachings that I just gave, though more expressive perhaps in the Islamic language, can be found in the Christian society.

RELIGION DEVELOPS OUR BEHAVIOR

RI: Then I assume that one of our real roles in humanity is to perfect our behavior, to have a better behavior towards other people and other national groups, other ethnic groups, and other social groups?

WDM: Certainly, that's the purpose of religion. It is to awaken the conscienceness of man; to make him see that it is good sense - not only is it charity or good deed, but it is good sense to be right by other people. Because when you're not right by other people, that has a damaging effect on you. Just to behave that way reinforces a spirit and an attitude that will eventually rob that person behaving that way of his or her own life and of good opportunities to live a good life in the future. You don't get happier by making other people unhappy.

RI: That kind of behavior will affect other people, and other people who are susceptible to those influences will cause it to spread.

WDM: Certainly.

RI: I guess that's how the spread of racism and many other evils also occur.

WDM: Yes. The Scripture says your death and your resurrection is "ka nas ta Wahida," is as one person or one soul. We understand that to mean that Adam slipped from the way, and then sin multiplied, wrongdoings multiplied and oppression came. And then whenever one turns the right way, God says to him "He turned." Adam himself turned according to the Qur'an. In the Bible it says that Jesus came before to fulfill the second Adam. But in the Qur'an it says that Adam himself turned. It says he met a Word from his Lord or he met with God's Word, and he turned. God accepted his repentance. As one man can represent what is the common life of all of us, then Adam represents the common natural life for all people. And that common natural life has the capacity to rise to the pinnacle or the highest degree of excellence in God's creation.

This comes because of an attitude agreeing with the best nature that God made for all people. And it is lost because of us going away from that attitude of complementing or of fulfilling the best nature that God created for us. So it's our attitude towards the better person in us that brings us up and brings us down.

RI: That reminds me of a verse in the Qur'an that says that Allah will never change the condition of a people, until they first can change that which is in their souls.

WDM: Yes, and it means their attitude. It says, until they change what is bothering their souls. That is an Arabic expression or a

Quranic expression. In English it simply means until they respond to the pricks in their conscience, or the voice that says "Come away from this bad life, and come away from these bad habits. Come away from this bad attitude." I don't care how far we get into crime, we never get so far into crime where the conscience does not rise up occasionally. So until we respond to the better mind or the better spirit in us, we will continue to suffer the consequences of our wrongdoings. And I have to repeat, that nobody can make their own situation better by making another person's situation bad. Eventually it hurts you more than it hurts those that you're trying to hurt.

THE HUMAN IS NOT A NATURAL SINNER

RI: The point that you brought up about how the Qur'an says Adam slipped, reminds me of how we were brought up basically thinking that because of Adam we were born in sin.

WDM: Well, that's the uniqueness of this religion. This religion says that man is NOT a natural sinner – that the natural impulse in man is the impulse towards excellence. This is Islamic teaching. The definition of a man is a RATIONAL BEING. That is what separates me from my dog, from a rabbit or any animal. I'm a rational being; I'm a reasoning being. I'm a being that is capable of making independent free choices. If I don't want to act like a human being, I don't have to. I'm free enough in my makeup and free enough to live a dog's life, if I want to. A dog cannot stand on his feet and talk like I'm talking. But if I want to, I can get on my hands and knees and bark like a dog and behave like a dog. So God has given me that freedom. But, is that my level? Is that what God created me to be? God has created me to be a human being, a thinking moral being.

You know human beings are the only creatures that cry. Yes, we cry tears. When we worry our hair turns grey. So we are unique beings. Allah has made us very uniquely human. And when we live on this plane, we're serving our nature. The impulse in me is the impulse to live on a human plane. My natural impulse is not to live on a dog plane. So if I become a dog now, and someone finds me living like a dog, they may say "look what God made." But God didn't make me that. God gave me the freedom to be that, and I came out of what God made me and became that.

So we say in Al-Islam that man has not been created to sin. His nature is to grow into human form; so his nature is not to sin but to grow towards morality and excellence. Excellent morals, excellent behavior, excellent senses is his natural destiny. So why should we say man is made to sin. I think many people have misunderstood even the Bible. I have read the Bible, too, and I have read what it says about sin, that sin is in the flesh and is natural. I have read all that. But I read the other things, too, that I think a lot of people perhaps are not reading. And I have come to the conclusion that the Bible is not saying that at all.

Allah has created human beings for excellence and the natural life of the human being is good and motivates or drives the human being towards more and more excellence. And when he comes out of that, he is out of his form. So what he does out of his form should not be charged against his form, but should be charged against his freedom, against his choice, and against his way of handling that freedom. I have the freedom to make choices outside of my own interest and outside of my own dignity. So if I make choices outside of that, charge it to my judgement and not to my nature. That was my "judgement" in the wrong, not my "nature."

TO FULFILL ALLAH'S PURPOSE

RI: Then, it would be true that Allah has really blessed man with the ability to control his own destiny.

WDM: We believe that man has been freed to make contributions to his destiny and to shape his own future. But we believe that Allah has already decided that man can only fulfill what Allah has made him capable of doing. And if he becomes great, it is because Allah supplied him with the instruments, with the tools and the faculties or whatever to do that and also to find an environment that invites him and supports him in reaching his great destiny. So we don't want to say "man controls his own destiny," without qualifying that. Yes, we do believe that man is free to work his own future out. But whatever he does, it is because of God's creation and His Generosity and Mercy.

RI: In the same sense then, if he lives the life that God has made for him to live, then he can reach his full potentials?

WDM: Yes. He's fulfilling his potential. But since God designed that and designed the world to favor that, he's also fulfilling God's purpose. So we can't say that man is shaping the future, or that he is working out the future for himself. Nor can we say that man is building or shaping his own destiny. We have to say that he is fulfilling his potential as God intended.

RI: Then if he does not follow the plan that Almighty God has set forth for him, do we say he is working against himself?

WDM: He certainly is. And the key is to know that you can't change the whole world. People have to remain free to choose the life they want. We cannot take that freedom away from people. But for the benefit of those who don't want to disgrace themselves and don't want to let down their excellence - for they want to respect their excellence in fulfilling it, if they can - for the benefit of those people, then we have to say that in order to fulfill your potential, you have to be motivated by good and by the desire to do good. We can't do that, if we're not motivated by the desire to be good.

With all of our genius, for some of us have great genius - no matter what we have, we can't progress the world in a good way that benefits everybody and brings about the release of that great potential in us as we want, unless we have the desire to do good. It is because if I don't have the desire to do good, as your potential starts to match mine, as your potential starts to unfold, and you begin to get credit along with me, and your name becomes as popular as mine - if I don't have that motivation to do good in me, then I will become jealous and begin to work against your potential. And if I work to hold down your potential, then eventually I become an oppressor - I'll hold down any man's potential.

So we have to try not to go away from the very simple things in religion. And that is that we should be motivated by the spirit to do good. Charity is not only a number one principle in Christianity, charity is also a number one principle for Muslims.

RI: Imam Muhammad, we thank you for the insight that you've given us.

WDM: Well, I'm only quoting. Praise be to Allah.

RI: We thank Allah for blessing us with this opportunity to get a better understanding of our religion. We thank you, our audience, for inviting us into your homes once again. Our program is titled "Al-Islam in Focus." We'd like to give you the greetings of all the prophets from Abraham to Muhammad — the greetings of peace in the Qur'an and Arabic language of As-Salaamu-Alaikum.

PART III

September 18, 1984

Our religion teaches us that we should be active and supportive of all the good things that a society has established. When Prophet Muhammad (PBUH) established the small society or the first community of Muslims in Medina, he guaranteed to Christians and Jews the freedom to practice their religion as they had practiced it before he came into leadership. He also required of them, whether they were Jews, Christians, or Sabians, that they support and contribute to the common needs of that new society.

         Imam W. Deen Mohammed

ان ديننا يأمرنا بان نكون متعاونين ومتكافلين بكل ماهو مشروع لاقامة مجتمعنا. ان الرسول صلى الله عليه وسلم : عندما انشأ أول مجتمع فى المدينه المنوره ضمن لباقي الديانات من اليهوديه والمسيحيه حريه العباده دون المساس بحرياتهم . وكذلك طلب منهم جميعاً ان يتعاونوا فيما بينهم بما فيهم المسلمين لكل الامور التي تهم جميعاً.

ہمارا دین ہمیں سکھاتا ہے کہ ہم ان اچھی چیزوں میں معاون و مددگار بنیں جو ہمارے سماج میں رائج ہیں ۔ جب حضرت محمد صلی اللہ علیہ وسلم نے مدینہ میں پہلی اسلامی سوسائٹی قائم کی تو انہوں نے یہود و نصاریٰ کو ان کی حقوق اور مذہبی آزادی کی مکمل ضمانت دی ۔ انہوں نے یہود و نصاریٰ اور صائبین کو یہ دعوت بھی دی کہ مذہبی اختلاف کے باوجود جدید سوسائٹی کی تعمیر و ترقی میں بھرپور حصہ لیں ۔

RI: As-Salaamu-Alaikum. Ladies and gentlemen, we would like to thank you very much for letting us come into your homes once again. The title of our program is Al-Islam in Focus. My name is Robert Islam. I'd like to introduce you to our leader, Imam W. Deen Muhammad. It is a priviledge to have him here again. As-Salaamu-Alaikum, Brother Imam.

WDM: Wa-Alaikum As-Salaam.

RI: I'd also like to introduce you to our co-host, Imam Mustafa Hassain. As-Salaamu-Alaikum Imam Hassain.

IMH: Wa-Alaikum As-Salaam.

RI: Ladies and gentlemen, I don't think that I could give a better introduction than a book that Imam Muhammad has written entitled *As the Light Shineth from the East*. And I'd like to read a few excerpts from the book as it speaks on W. Deen Muhammad:

"He stressed the need for inter-racial, inter-cultural and inter-religious encounter. He spoke of the Islamic respect for Jesus and expressed the hope that the Christians would visit his community for his new series of jubilees. He said that the Christians and Muslims should together give witness to the religious values we share. That we should stop being concerned with labels. Adding that he wanted to see Christians as better Christians and Muslims as better Muslims, rather than trying to convert each other." — Dr. John Taylor, World Council of Churches.

"He showed great courage when, since 1975 as the leader of the American Muslim Mission, he turned his movement around and gave it a new inspired direction. He called for cooperation instead of strife between Jewish, Christian and Muslim leaders and people. He called for cooperation with the common front against drunkenness and against the ever-progressing destruction of family in the United States. And we are with him all the way in this fight. It is our fight as well.

We think that the combined moral power of the major faiths should be felt more in our society. Each one of us alone is a voice in the wilderness, and together we shall be heard." — Senior Rabbi Joshua O'Haberman, Washington Hebrew Congregation.

"I believe that he is a genuine vital religious leader, who I believe that his power to do what he has done in such a short time is a power that comes from God. In lecture appearances all over the world he has stated strong resistance to any form of leadership that hides the truth and rips off the people. He has managed to help change much in the attitude of those who deny proper opportunity to women today. He shows our common faith is one that commands us to stand against political or religious injustice or disservice to truth in whatever form. He is a sign of our times, a sign of the direction in which God is leading all of us." — Father Lawrence Parkhurst, Resident Priest, Sacred Heart Catholic Church, Flint, Michigan.

ISLAMIC POLITICAL AWARENESS

Ladies and gentlemen, we would now like to begin our interview with our leader. Imam Muhammad, recently you started a series of political awareness seminars across the country. We just attended one in New York. What do you really hope to accomplish by these seminars that you're starting?

WDM: Yes, Brother Islam. As you are aware, the community that I represent at one time didn't believe as we believe now. And during those days prior to February, 1975, there was hardly any political involvement at all on the part of our members. We know that there was an indication that the Honorable Elijah Muhammad would support at Black candidate of his choice, he said if he saw in the candidate the things that he would expect in a candidate for the Black people. Not very much happened or came from that. But I believe he was referring to the congressman from New York, Adam Clayton Powell, who has passed some time ago. I think he admired something in Adam Clayton Powell, for he was a strong leader in Harlem.

The Honorable Elijah Muhammad, himself, helped us to make

the kind of program that we are making now. Because many of his followers, I believe, are supporting us because they feel that we are really going not only in the direction that the Qur'an religion requires us to go in, but they also feel that even though the Honorable Elijah Muhammad represented something quite different from what we believe in now in terms of the religious concept, that he intended for us to move into the mainstream of life. Not as a civil rights movement, but as people who need to get something for themselves and something of real value and consequence in this country. So to do that he felt that one day it would be necessary for some political involvement.

However, as Muslims, we feel obligated, and our religion teaches us that we should be active and supportive of all the good things that a society has established. The Prophet Muhammad, peace and blessing be upon him, when he established the small society or the first community of Muslims in Medina, he guaranteed to Christians and Jews the freedom to practice their religion as they had practiced it before he came into the leadership there and before the Muslims gained control of that society. He also required of them, whether they were Jews, Christians, or Sabians, that they support and contribute to the common needs of that new society that was formed.

What I'm referring to exactly is the need for all citizens to contribute to the welfare of the state. So they had to pay a tax and had to share the burden of taxes. And they had to share the burden of defense for Medina, whether they were Muslims or not. They were all supposed to unite against a common enemy. If Medina was attacked by a common enemy they were all supposed to share that responsibility. And I would say, there are other supports for us also from the history of Prophet Muhammad, peace be upon him, and in the Qur'an that says that if a Muslim state requires of non-Muslim citizens a participation in the support for the general welfare of that state, then if a Muslim is in a non-Muslim state, he should accept to do the same. He is obligated to support the general welfare of the state that he's in, if that state permits him the same thing that the Muslim state permitted non-Muslims, Christians and Jews and Sabians. If it permits him to practice his religion, if it does not persecute him because of his religion, and it permits him to live his Muslim life in the country, then the Muslim should feel obligated to support the structures or the establishment of that particular society. I'm talking about the educational institutions, the political processes of government, etc.

So we feel that we are obligated as Muslims to get involved, and these seminars are really a way of encouraging Muslims to take a real part in the political process and to become better educated as citizens. Because a big part of it is citizenship education. And we know that too many Blacks are going to the polls and are just voting for the first time, that is many of them. And many times they feel insecure or inadequate. It's simply because they haven't gone through the simple training of how to carry out the processes of voting in the voting booth or at the voting station. So a big part of the political awareness program is just to give simple instructions and educate the members who are just beginning now to participate in the voting process. But the other part of it, which I think is more important to us, is to encourage aggressiveness on the part of the Muslim members – aggressiveness in the terms of aspiring for positions in government and accepting to support worthy leaders, whether they are Muslims or non-Muslims, who are aspiring for positions in government.

IN DEFENSE OF THE NATION

RI: Yes sir. Brother Imam, that brings up this point. In America today, under the way that we live, then being able to practice our religion freely and to grow into the way America is, then regarding the armed forces, if we're attacked as an American country, should the Muslims go join the armed forces to support this country?

WDM: Well, I can't order people. But I believe that the life that we all value as Americans is worthy of our willing support. We don't want to force anyone or order anyone to accept their responsibility for the defense of the nation. But we speak for ourselves. If I had it to do all over again, with my understanding of the religion and my duties as a Muslim, in a state that permits me to live my religion and practice my religion freely, I would accept to be enlisted and go to war in defense of this country.

COLOR CONSCIOUS FEELINGS CAN BURDEN AFRICAN-AMERICAN PEOPLE

RI: With the political situation what it is today, how do you see the African-American community? Do we need more political awareness as a body of people?

WDM: Yes sir. I do believe that. And it's because we're not just Americans. We are Americans with a unique history of inequality, disadvantage, slavery, etc. It is a condition that is in the past, but many of us are still suffering some effects of slavery. Also during the days of Jim-Crowism in this country, I think many of us had been so intimidated by the overwhelming forces that were threatening to deny us equal opportunity in this country or equal recognition as citizens, that it has been passed on to us by our grandparents and parents. And still some of us feel that our color is a burden on us. That just being Black in America is a burden that we have to carry.

I don't feel that, not in these days. I don't feel that my color is a burden for me. But I know we'll have a lot of opposition. People will say, "Well how can you prove that? The color is an opposition. The color is a burden on us. We are Black. We are treated differently." Certainly we are treated differently. But if you don't accept that anyone has a right to treat you differently, that there is no one with the right to deny you justice in this country, and as long as the law protects you, I think you shouldn't feel any burden. In fact, this can work for us, because we know that people under pressure usually perform in a way that surprises themselves.

I don't think this little pressure that we have in the United States necessarily has to be a negative for us. It can be turned into a plus. And many of us have turned it into a plus. We are continuing a line of progression that our nobel ancestors set for us who didn't accept slavery and didn't accept to be treated as an inferior human being. And in spite of the conditions of slavery and of segregation in this country, they made progress and they left that legacy to us. They accomplished much because of their courage to meet the challenge and demand their rights.

Now with the government taking the position that it has taken for some years now, and with the law of the land working as much for us as it works for anybody else, sometimes we have people saying it works too much for us now – that we're the favorite. I don't know about that, for I still think the country is obligated to take a very strong stand in the defense of Black people's rights to equality and equal opportunity in this country. And sometimes it seems that we are being favored, but that's necessary until the attitudes of the citizens of this country conform to what is best for the whole country.

All I want to say is we are free people in this country, and the courts of the land will protect our rights. All we have to do is realize that and stop feeling that just because we are black, we're easily identified because of our color. So a White Irish can move around, and nobody knows him as an Irish. I think that's an excuse we should put down now, and we should just accept our responsibility as citizens and just move right in, accept the challenge, seize the opportunity, and go forward.

RI: Do you feel that because we accepted the attitude of being a second-class citizen, that it kind of works against us?

WDM: Yes, you can't accept that. If you accept that, then you are already defeated.

BALANCED LEADERSHIP

RI: I know this is a presidential year. What do you look for in political leadership, a person qualifying for the presidential office?

WDM: Let us look at another thing first. The ward chairman, the local man in the neighborhod who works with city government to pass on to the laborers information, etc. that is helpful to them, and who communicates for the neighbors with the government on behalf of the neighbors that person is in a small position when we think of the presidency of the United States. But even a small role like that, we require of that person a degree of integrity.

As we move higher, then the moral responsibilities become greater. And not only the moral responsibilities become greater, but the sensitivities have to be bigger. One who aspires for the office of the President of the United States has to be able to appreciate the good that they see in every citizen. And they have to be able to respond to the needs of any citizen. So if an Hispanic becomes President of the United States, and it is possible, because they say by the year 2000 maybe they will be the biggest minority. And it is possible that one day we'll have an Hispanic as the President of the United States – that Hispanic will have to be able to serve the needs of all Americans. That Hispanic will have to be aware of his affiliation with his own ethnic group. But once he begins to aspire for the office of the President of the United States, he has to show some kind of balance and not favor his own ethnic group that much, or not represent the concerns of his ethnic group so much that he makes other ethnic groups fear that he can't represent their concerns. So I would look for principle and broadmindedness, bigheartedness and kindness, and love for everybody. I look for those things to be in a man that wants that office, along with the qualifications that he would need to do the practical job.

MINISTER FARRAKHAN AND REVEREND JESSE JACKSON?

RI: In a recent interview in *Newsweek* Magazine, it was stated that you felt that Minister Farrakhan and Jesse Jackson both are liars and hypocrites. Was that an accurate report?

WDM: If I say at one time in this interview that a certain individual or public figure is a liar, and then later on in the interview, maybe about ten or fifteen minutes later, I say that a certain individual is a hypocrite – they double those up, put them right together, and it is not quite the way it was given. But here is what I was saying. I was saying that the Reverend Jesse Jackson is not just a candidate for the office of President, he is also a Reverend. He should represent Christianity too. And we know him as a Reverend. We don't know him yet as a President. So we should expect him to present himself in a manner that would command respect from sensitive Christians, Christians who are sensitive to the needs or to those qualities that should be reflected in a personality that says he is a minister or a reverned. And I would think that that person would have to be concern to stay in line with what is most essential for him as a Christian person. I think that is what is most essential for a Christian minister, that he doesn't violate the essential principles or the basic teachings of his own religion or put himself in a position where people will question or doubt his loyalty to his own principles.

I see in the Reverend Jesse Jackson a desperation, and his association with Minister Farrakhan and in including people like that shows that. Let's go back to something earlier. You remember the march on Washington? Wasn't something missing in terms of purity or consistency in this last march, when we compare it to the march that was led by Dr. King?

RI: Yes sir.

WDM: We knew what the march led by Dr. King was about. It was clear what those marchers were marching for. But this last march had everything in it. It looked like they were desperate to get numbers, and just everything came into that march. Not that I can't accept women's rights. I accept women's rights. Even the Hare Krishna people, and these small minority religious groups that come from Asia have rights. I recognize them. They're entitled to that. But is this a march of all underdogs, all underprivileged people in the country? Are we forgetting the central and main concern? And that is the Black history and the Black needs. I think if they're going to march in the name of Black people, then they shouldn't bring all these other things in that confuse the picture. That was a sign of desperation.

Again, they wanted 200,000 marchers. And if they have to get them from the woods and from Broadway and from back alleys, no matter where they come from, they would get these numbers. When a reverend starts pulling in a man that represents something that is in direct conflict with what the church represents, then I think that again is an indication of desperation on his part. And it's not becoming of a Christian minister or Christian principle, or a person who claims to be a good Christian of principle. So I would say I was justified in saying that a minister is a hypocrite when he associates with people that represent something that is in direct conflict with his finest principles, with the most essential principles of Christianity. Here is a man who is in direct conflict with those principles, and now he was asking him to help him get votes. Something is wrong there.

THE ECONOMIC ROLE OF AMERICA HAS CHANGED

RI: In the economical situation that we see today, what is the position of the African-American in the economical situation of the world?

WDM: The economic situation of the world today is one of, I would think, a demand for restraint and optimum productivity on the part of the citizens of the world. No more can America – and authorities are telling us this – expect to benefit fom the markets of the peoples of the world, from the resources of the world as it once did. Before, the world was not industrialized as it is now, and then the third world was not asking for industrialization. But they're asking for more now. Their appetites have been excited, and America has been one of the main factors in exciting the appetites of the undeveloped nations. So those undeveloped nations are not going to accept now that they don't get their share of their own resources. Because of that, now America is not as powerful and not as great an influence in the world, speaking in terms of an industrial nation. America's place has been changed; America's role in the international world has been changed drastically. And America is looking now to see what kind of help it can give these countries to help them develop industry and to help them come up.

Because of that the citizens of America just can't expect material plenty in their lives. This is an affluent nation, and I believe it will continue to be an affluent nation, a nation with plenty. But we can't expect the same amount of wealth in the lives of the American people. We're going to have to accept to live more in line with our means. We cannot afford all this show of wealth that's not supported by anything. We can't expect anymore job programs with nothing to back them up, with no real resources and with no real production to back them up. We can't expect that anymore.

No matter whether we have a Republican or a Democrat in the White House, these realities have to be accepted. So I think the African-American situation economically has greatly changed. He's going to have to be more productive. He can't expect a lot of handouts or someone to take care of him, while he just remains idle. That's good for America and good for Blacks, the African-Americans.

MORAL LEADERSHIP IS AN ESSENTIAL OBLIGATION

RI: Do you want to add to that, Imam Hassain?

IMH: I wanted to get back to this point of belief, when you said that we don't believe like we used to. And I think that in the days of the Honorable Elijah Muhammad, we can compare it with bringing up a child. A lot of people think that because we don't believe like we used to believe, that somethig is going wrong. But to me, that stimulates growth and development. Because a child thinks in certain stages of his growth and development in one way, and then as he grows with more understanding, his thinking changes, his belief in things change, and he is thinking of change. Now, what you are saying is very important to me, because as I see the political situation and the old way of politicians campaigning for the role in office they went out more or less to pacify the people and to talk about what the people wanted. They make a platform on that, instead of getting at what the people actually needed.

As he has asked you the question of what kind of leader did you look for, and what qualifications did you believe that this leader should have, goes right back to good moral character. But if he comes out with the people believing and thinking in that old way of politics, then they would only be looking for a man that would help them in their material gain, more or less, like getting jobs. Right now we know jobs are scarce. And when a politician goes out now, he tells the people that he's going to open up jobs, so that they can get back in the way of life that they've been. My question is since we know that moral character would be the qualification of a good politician or a good leader or a good representative in any area, then where do we start?

WDM: That's a very difficult question. Because you know the moral background of candidates is hardly ever known by people, by the public, unless there is something awfully terrible in the history of that person. And then his opponents usually dig it up and bring it out. But many times they're afraid to do that, because they have similar kinds of problems for themselves. I think we should be able to help the common citizens. We all have an obligation. In our religion the strong have an obligation to help the weak. The learned have an obligation to aid the unlearned, until they become educated or sufficiently educated to manage for themselves. So in our religion, the strong and the educated and the capable people are obligated to assist others that are less fortunate. I think we should carry out that responsibility, and that is the purpose of the seminars on political awareness. So that we can extend a capable hand of help to persons who are less fortunate; help them educate themselves, so they'll be able to make wise choices. Something that we should be aware of is that God has equipped every human being. Any person that's not suffering any serious mental damage or mental empairment, and if they have their wits, then they don't have to be educated.

God has given us a moral sense of what is right and wrong. Most of us, if we would be moral ourselves, we can detect when a person is immoral. And I think what we should look for in a candidate is a desire to serve the good of the society and to serve the needs of individuals, whether it be the need for jobs, or a need for moral strength in their lives, or the need for family discipline. We should look for a person who can evidence to us a desire to serve. And that will be known. If you don't see the desire to serve, it's going to be evident and very obvious that that person has a desire for power and has a desire to be recognized for personal gain. We will see vanity, and we will see greed for power. We will see the love of the limelight, a desire for a control over people. And we don't have to be that educated to see these things in people, because a human being is equipped with this sensitive monitor in his body. A good heart can find these things and recognize these things. So I think what we should do is make the public aware that situations of, I would say, inability to move forward, situations of stagnation — these situations are very frustrating. And they can become so frustrating that they create desperation in the public. And that's the time we're living in right now. We're living in a time where the world has just leaped so fast and so far ahead that many of us, because we feel ourselves inadequate and we feel ourselves short-changed, are suffering a condition of extreme desperation. And in a situation like this you don't think straight, and you don't see straight. You just go along with anybody just to relieve some of that frustration or just to prove a point. That's what we should be aware of. That we are living in desperate times, and many of us are burdened by desperation. That means that we should give more thought of what is best for us in terms of our own personal behavior and involvement, and don't jump on any bandwagon just because it's making a noise, or just because it gives us an opportunity to express some of our anxieties or relieve some of the frustration in us, or express some of our grievances. That's not enough.

We don't want to go forward with a campaign that's just a grievancy campaign. A grievancy campaign alone is going to make us forget what the real purpose should be, or it will make us undo the good works that we have taken so much pain to do. We don't want to create an image of ourselves that will discredit us or take away our legitimacy. We are African-American people, I believe, continuing to follow the better aspirations of our people up from slavery. And we wouldn't want to discredit that and present an African-American community that would follow a demagogue or follow anyone who expressed the rage of the Black community. It's not enough to express the rage of the Black community. We have to have people that will be responsible to the Black community and not undo the good works we have done. We do not want to take away the legitimacy of the African-American people's protest.

THE COURAGE OF
THE HONORABLE ELIJAH MUHAMMAD
FROM DUST TO INDUSTRY

RI: You had established a program called AMMCOP, the American-Muslim Mission Committee to Purchase 100,000 Commodities plus. AMMCOP was better known as the co-operative buying. How does this program compare with the econmic blueprint that the Honorable Elijah Muhammad established?

WDM: I would like to think that we were actually continuing in that line of progress, in that direction. We have had many leaders who have believed that it's not enough to leave the African-American economic situation to natural happenings. That just like the political situation needs a special effort; we believe that the economic situation requires special effort. And that means an organized effort and a collective effort. The Honorable Elijah Muhammad was, as you know, very big in his thinking. And he was a man of great courage in light of his stature and knowing that he was not a college graduate. We have to acknowledge him as maybe one of the greatest African-American persons we have in our history, when it comes to addressing material and economic needs, and also moral needs of the little man or of the ordinary African-

American person. We would like to feel that we are continuing in that tradition of requiring courage, of courageous acts on the part of small people.

I think when you ask small people to build factories, you're really asking for a courageous act. It is a courageous act to tell poor people, "Let's build a factory. Let us have our own factories, and let us put our small earnings together and save. Let us put these small savings together, so that one day we'll have a transportation line, a trucking line." That's what the Honorable Elijah Muhammad did. He preached that to the poor Black man, the African-American people, who were in a poverty situation. So that's great courage, and what we're doing is continuing in that tradition. It's necessary, until we have a sufficient number of African-American poor people accepting to be gainfully employed, accepting their responsibility to themselves, to create conditions and opportunities when there's no opportunity. Just like right now, there are no jobs for many of us.

We don't have to accept that. There are things that we can do together. There are still services that can be rendered. There are still needs out there in the community. And I believe that we should not be satisfied to let people from across town come into our community and sell us everything that we need, and do everything for us. That's not right. We should be creative. We should be imaginative. And we should be able to take circumstances like this, turn it around, and make it work for us. And the proof that it can be done was what we did under the Honorable Elijah Muhammad. It was a group of poor people, but look how we bought thousands of acres of land, and had a fish business and imports/exports business. And right now in Atlanta, the brothers there have twelve fast-food businesses, and they are buying fish together, collectively, and realizing a good business. And we want to keep that up.

If the Haitians, the Cubans, the Koreans, and Asians can come over here and get a little store and work hard, and eventually turn it into a successful business, then why can't we do the same? We've been over here in America longer then they have. We should know the ropes better then they do. We should be able to get support from the American people for our constructive work and for our courage as a poor people or a poor community. We should get help, too. And believe me, we would get more help from the

American people, than the Asians are getting. But we won't get it accepting the condition of welfare for the great numbers of the African-American people.

DEVELOPING A MODEL OF ISLAMIC EXCELLENCE IN AMERICA

RI: Imam Muhammad, I know that we had a farm in Georgia, and that we also had a school in Sedalia. I know that with the conditions that exist in the city today, which are very tedious because of the crime and other things, the last time that we spoke you spoke of the plans you wished could have been implimented on the Georgia farm.

WDM: Yes. We had better than 4000 acres of land that were acquired by the followers of the late Honorable Elijah Muhammad by poor people putting their little pennies and dollars together under his leadership. And we had managed to finish paying off the mortgage. The land was clear. All we had to do is pay taxes. We still hold hopes that the probate courts will clear us, and release that land to the community. Right now it's in question. The probate courts are holding the land in question. The opposition is trying to say, and the courts have been seen as favoring the oppostion, that that land might have been the private property of the Honorable Elijah Muhammad. Now you know not and only Muslims know better than that, but the public knows better than that. Christian African-Americans and Whites that have read of us, they know better than that. So if they pull that off, that will really be a disgrace.

We hold out hopes to get that land into our possession and utilize it for the purpose of building a smaller model of Muslim excellence in this country. We would like to have a collective farming community, where there would be maybe three acres or so owned by each person. And they'll have their home on that acreage of as much as five acres or ten acres or more mayube for some of them. But we don't want to give big acreage to any one person, because we'd like more people to share in that program and project. We hope to have mosques for our religious services and school there. We want to have what they used to call in the pioneer's day the central store, where you go and get your needs, where there is garden tools, blue jeans, shoes and whatever. We hope to have that. We hope to one day have our own city services, small town services like a fire department, et ceteria. We hope to build a little model town. And we have great enthusiam. We have a great amount of spirit and enthusiasm in our community for that venture.

Also we had, as you mentioned, the land in Sedalia. (Since this interview, the Sedalia property was taken by the probate court.) If we have to give up anything, I would hope it may be a percentage of the acreage in Georgia to the heirs of the Honorable Elijah Muhammad. But they have us in such confusion, that we can't expect all that we think justice should give us. They have us over the barrel, so to speak, because of confused handling of funds, et cetera by the Nation of Islam in those days.

We have many who have made application to move out of the cities. Some will sell their homes where they are in the northern cities, and from the sale of their homes they would have enough money to buy economy housing, a home tailored to their need, to their pocketbook and to their resources. And they most likely will have money left over from the sale of their home in the city to put into a savings account. So they'll have a home and a savings, whereas now they just have a home and bills in the North. You are right, life is very tedious for us living in big cities.

African-American people, because of their almost total absence of any productivity on their part in a manner of speaking, don't represent a tax base for the city. This puts our city officials in a very precarious situation, and it weakens the city. We think there is a better chance for us if we move out. We don't want everybody to do it, but a sufficient number and a select group should move from these big burdened cities to a place where our costs of living would be considerably reduced for us. Then we can make a real investment in a better situation in small towns, and we can come back to the city and preach redemption.

RI: When I was speaking with you earlier, you were saying that a lot of the settled people would be willing to do this. I know that my wife and I are not settled yet, but just for the opportunity to get out of this city situation and be able to produce and do things for ourselves, we would move.

WDM: We want a settled people, but they don't have to be settled in the sense of being established. We mean sober.

THE WOMAN'S ROLE IS THE FOUNDATION OF GOVERNMENT

RI: I'm glad you clarified that. Imam, I know recently you were in New York at the Political Awareness Seminar, and Imam Hassain made a comment that there were so many women and children there. He would like to make a comment about that now.

IMH: Not getting away from AMMCOP and the farm, but all this ties in together. It goes to the very root of the good family life. And family life seems to be the thing that has been broken up, that has caused many of the problems. Now at this seminar there was a very strong feeling. And I asked you a few minutes ago about where do we start to get back to this moral base that we have to come up from. I have visited many national meetings like this. And I saw an overwhelming majority of women with the youth and even small children. This moved me, because I really believe strongly that that's the key – our women getting back in their family structure with the children and bringing these ideas of leadership home that should take place in the political leader, the educators, the scientists and all the rest of the people that have to do with leadership of humanity. What I want to ask Imam Muhammad is would he elaborate on some of the points regarding the overwhelming majority of women and children that came out.

WDM: Yes sir. Accounting for the greater number of women with children at the affair, I think is the hope that they now have because of the position that their men have taken. The Political Awareness Seminars and the AMMCOP people who were involved in making that a success understand the role of these efforts. We believe that political involvement or political awareness without an awareness of the need for some material production or some material acquisition will be nothing. It will be weak. That's the situation for us in the big cities right now. We have a lot of voters with us, but our candidates can't expect much from us in terms of financial support. And it's certainly because we have not established ourselves business-wise and economically. As the effort is not only an effort to inform our citizens of the political processes and to help them become more effective or involved in that process, the effort is also to show that the two have to be brought along together. That is an effort to improve our material life as well as to improve our involvement in the political process of America.

I think the women are now beginning to see hope. They're saying, "Our men now know what we need." They're saying they're going to get some food on the table, and they're going to also be involved politically. So this is a real ray of hope in our lives, and I think that's why we're seeing the women coming out with their children. Because they're the ones who are most in need of a productive man. A woman with no children doesn't have as much need for a productive man as a woman with children. So that's why we're seeing these women out here. That's the main reason for it. But, I think something else is very important here. If these women now are going to get involved, women with children, what we're going to see is a change in the home environmment. Because if these women come out and put themselves on the line and say, "Yes, I want to be supportive; I want to get involved here; I want to help." Then that's going to give them a better image in the eyes of their children. It's going to make them more supportive of their husbands who are struggling. And I think we're going to see stronger families, stronger African-American families because of their involvement.

LEADERSHIP FOR THE HOME IS THE WOMAN'S ROLE

IMH: Yes, and that's going to strengthen the man. That's going to give him the moral support that he needs to move ahead and get these accomplishments.

WDM: It certainly will. In fact, it has already strengthened me, seeing those women out their with their children. We talked about that, and you brought out that point. That no matter how much a man desires to, he just can't take a mother's responsibility over. The child knows mother. If the father just says, ";Okay, go upstairs and wash and go to bed," he has to get the child upstairs with a strap or a threat. The child starts looking at mama, right away. And if mama doesn't give that support, dad may have to use that strap. And that's not the way you want it. In our religion the woman is responsible for the children being brought up as Muslims and being brought up as healthy citizens of society. The woman is responsible for that.

The man is responsible for helping her and to provide her with the means – living quarters, clothing for the children, money for education if it's acquired, et cetera. Allah says the men are maintainers for women, and maintaining them means just what Allah said. He said that He had given men a degree over women in terms of their physical strength and their acquisition of wealth. That they should spend out of their wealth for the maintenance of women, and they should use their physical strength to bring that bread in. So, I think we should understand as men that there's only so much we can do to get the discipline that we want in our children. If that's not coming mainly from that mother, then we are going to create a hell for ourselves in that house by going against her. We can't go against her. We have to support her, and she should support us. We want and need the women to be with us.

MOTHER — THE FIRST WOMB OF LIFE

IMH: That means that it would be pretty difficult actually for a man to even get to the child, unless he comes through the woman. And also the child cannot get to the man, unless he comes through the woman.

WDM: That's true. The children are under their mother, and God has made it that way. And you're right, all of us come through the woman. We don't get there any other way.

THE ROLE OF THE MAN AND WOMAN IN AL-ISLAM

RI: Imam Muhammad, could you define for us the role of the man and woman in the Muslim society. Many of our viewers would like to know how the man and the woman in the Muslim society live.

WDM: There have been some recent discussions of the role of the Muslim man and woman by scholars from the Islamic world, Saudi Arabia, in association with an university in America. The traditional role of the man in Muslim society is that of a bread-winner for the family and a support for the mother as the supervisor and authority in the home. The man in Al-Islam is careful not to take from that authority. He respects the wife as the mother, and whatever he does before the children, he does it in such a way that they see that he recognizes the woman as being responsible for the home environment – the cleanliness of the home, the order of the home, the choice of meals, and everything in the household.

But more important than even that, perhaps, is her responsibility as the first teacher in the house. She is responsible to feed the appetite of her child with the healthy kinds of cultural influences and to encourage the child, to excite the mental appetite or the intellectual appetite of that child. She is the first one responsible for exciting the intellectual appetite of the child. She should keep healthy materials in the environment, once the child becomes of age where he can start to read. She is supposed to help him learn to read. She is supposed to be the first teacher of reading to her child.

She, in fact, from the very first day of the birth of the child should begin saying to the child words of the Qur'an. She should recite Al-Fatihah to the child, so that the child right away hears the revelation of God in the environment from the very first day of the birth, even when the baby's born. She begins right away when she receives the child or when the child is delivered from her; she gets the child in her arms, says Al-Fatihah, with the Name of Allah, Most Gracious, Most Compassionate to the end, in the ears of the child. When she's nursing the child or caring for the child, she should recite verses from Qur'an so that the child hears the Qur'an in Arabic language. Or if she can't do it in Arabic, she should do it in English so the child hears the message of the Revelation, the Message of the Qur'an. As the child grows older, as I said, she should find healthy learning materials to bring into the environment so the child's mind will be groomed right and the intellectual curiosities will be awakened and helped along. She is the teacher. She is clean in her house, and she is a teacher. She is responsible for that home environment.

She is even responsible for supporting the man in his moral and spiritual needs. Not that she should ever assume a position of boss over her husband, but she should in a kind way and a supportive way remind him of his moral neglect. But not before the children; it should be done in privacy. She should remind him of his moral needs as his closest friend, as his closest companion, as one who has invested her life and her resources in partnership with that man. So she should support his good moral life and his good spiritual life. She should come to his rescue, when she sees that he needs support from her or support from society. She should come to his rescue and strengthen him in his determination to shoulder his responsibility as breadwinner of the family. She should strengthen him in his desire to be a support for society at large. What I mean by that is that she should look after his needs, too. And she should offer her help as a friend, as his closest friend and closest companion. Again, she should offer her help as a person, who has invested as a partner with her husband.

THE CORRECT IMAGE FOR THE MAN AND WOMAN

RI: Brother Imam, then the man's role, as you said earlier, is the maintainer and the provider. He's like the legs for the family.

WDM: Yes he is. He is expected as a Muslim in our religion to see that that woman is not wanting for support, male support, in her household. And male support means that he accepts responsibilities. We know the nature of society today and how it's almost impossible for one poor man to take care of a family by himself of four or five family members. We know that if a woman can earn some money, then it's badly needed now that she does something too to bring more money into the family. But the Muslim man doesn't want that situation in his life. That's not a situation that he can tolerate. But we don't want families to think that now they have to change that, and that the wife can't work anymore. What we would hope is that women would find a way to earn money at home, so they wouldn't have to go outside the home environment when they have little children. If they don't have little children, it's a different situation. If the children are all grown and gone, and the woman's freer from that responsibility now, well she can go into some profession, if she has the ability to. Or she can help her husband establish himself in some profession or some business, because the children are out of the way. The children are all taken care of, her obligation to them now is not taxing. So she could do it. But if she has little children, it is expected that she put her children before career ambitions and before social image. The best social image of a woman with children is success at home with her children.

FAMILY RIGHTS IN THE HOLY QUR'AN AND THE LIFE OF PROPHET MUHAMMAD

RI: Well, how was the family role originally established in Al-Islam?

WDM: It was established like every other role for us was established. It was established by Qur'an, the Word of God, and Sunnah of the Prophet or by what the Prophet, himself, established for us. And whatever he established, it has its support, its base in Qur'an, the Word of God. There are specific verses in Qur'an that tell us man's obligation.

Man's obligation is to defend society. Defending society means also not just going to war against an enemy nation or world, but it means also defending the material life of society. So if a Muslim man is not employed, or he is not responsible for some business or something, then he is not really fulfilling his life as A Muslim. So to fulfill his life as a Muslim, he has to be productive. He has to be employed and enjoying income from lawful employment. He has to improve that. He has to seek to be more effective and more useful to society in the material field. And he has to educate and seek improvement in his education. The Muslim man has to seek improvement in his own education, and he is obligated to see that his children receive an education.

In those days we call Jahaliyya of Arabia or a dark age for ignorant Arabians, the idea of education as we understand it today was none existent. So Prophet Muhammad, peace and blessings be upon him, obligated men to do something about educating their daughters. Men in those days took pride in male children, because males would go to war for them; males would help them plow the land, and would help them in their business. They didn't take much pride in female children as support for society. But Prophet Muhammad required of men that they should help their daughters get an education. Allah says in the Qur'an that education is an obligation for both the male and female child born. And Prophet Muhammad said if any male would educate two daughters, God would give him the paradise.

So this is a great encouragement that Prophet Muhammad gave the males, to educate and to be instrumental in promoting the intellectual cultivation of the females. Now why would the Qur'an, Allah's Word, and Prophet Muhammad put this heavy importance or significance on educating the women, if all they were going to do was have babies? So those who think that the society of Muslims is a society that oppresses the women, they don't understand the Qur'an, and they don't understand Prophet Muhammad's rule, the Messenger of God, peace be upon him. We have to understand this.

To address the role of women in international Muslim society, we have to understand that Muslim society or the world Muslim society has for centuries been under foreign domination, and just recently realized independence. A very small part of the Islamic world has escaped foreign domination. And with independence comes a need to restore the Islamic character and the Islamic life. So that process is going to be very slow. Those who dominated the Muslim land, who did not believe in the religion of Al-Islam, quite naturally feared the influences of Al-Islam in the life of Muslims. And they did everything they could to weaken that influence. Along with that came the setting back of the advancement for women in society, and also the diminishing role of the man in public life and in industry. You see a lack of industry in most of the Islamic world, and you see a need to bring the woman up in the culture of their society to give her a better image in cultural environment.

In Pakistan and a few other countries or nations I can name, the woman is realizing her dignity as a woman because some of them are over institutions. They are in medicine; they are in education; they are in many professional fields, and they are represented there. But still, the majority of the Muslim world has yet to come up. But I think with the recovery of Muslim life after the colonialization of Islamic nations, we are going to see along with the growth of business and industry and just general cultivation of their environment – we're going to see the return of the woman's role in Al-Islam.

In Prophet Muhammad's time the women were encouraged to participate in the political life as well. The women were told that if their political leaders or their governmental leaders deviate or show weakness, if they caused weakness in the Muslim society, that they had the right to speak up; they had a voice. In fact, there is a case where one woman corrected the great leader, Khalifah Omar, and he promised her that he would act immediately on the situation she pointed out to him. He accepted the responsibility that she charged him with, and something was done, because of that woman speaking out and voicing her grievances, voicing her complaint to the ruler, Omar. Omar, as you know, may God be pleased with him, was a Companion of Prophet Muhammad, and he took over the leadership of the Muslim society after Abu-Bakr, who was the first Khalifah after Prophet Muhammad.

So the family life is perhaps the most precious concern in a Muslim society. Allah makes obligations to our families our first duty. When it comes to charity, when it comes to sharing our money, we have to first look at our family needs. And we can't leave crying babies at home or a desperate mother at home and take our monies out and give it to some other concern. We have to take care of the home concerns. This is an obligation in the Muslim family. And if we understand it, even the most sacred concepts in Muslim life address the need for strong families. In other words, family life is sacred to Muslims.

RI: Imam Muhammad, we certainly enjoyed our interview with you, and we are very pressed for time. But we want you to know that we enjoyed you very much. We would like to let our public know, this is our Leader, W. Deen Muhammad. Along with me is our co-host, Imam Mustafa Hassain. We would like to give you the greetings from all the prophets from Abraham to Muhammad, the greetings of peace in the Qur'an and Arabic language, As-Salaamu-Alaikum.

WDM: Wa-Alaikum As-Salaam.

PART IV

September 18, 1984

I believe when African-American individuals or families learn more about our religion, they are going to see that our religion is more "demanding." And strong African-American people want something more demanding. They don't want something that says you can just relax, lay down and die or stay at home and nurse that adult size baby bottle and wait for the welfare check. We don't want to make our men soft and unprepared for the challenge of life in the world.

Imam W. Deen Mohammed

انني اعتقد بان العائلات او الافراد الافرو. امريكيه عندما تسمع عن ديننا فانها تجد ان ديننا يتطلب اشياء كثيره. وان هذه الفئه من الناس تحتاج لدين يطلب منهم المزيد، انهم لا يحتاجون ان يجلسوا في بيوتهم حيث يتوفر لهم كل شيء بما فيها الضمان الاجتماعي دون بذل ادنى مجهود وانما نريد من هذه الفئه من الناس ان تكون مستعده لمواجهه الصعاب التي تواجهها في العالم

AFRICAN-AMERICANS TURNING TO AL-ISLAM

RI: Imam, in a recent article in "American Muslim Journal" (now the "Muslim Journal") you felt that in the near future a great majority of African-Americans will accept Al-Islam as their religion. What are the factors that you feel are contributing to this situation?

WDM: Well, I find that the life of the African-American since he has been in America favors the African-Americans choosing our religion of the Muslims over the church and Christianity. These are just developments that work, I believe, in the favor of conversion to Al-Islam rather than to Christianity. I think a lot of us are not yet acquainted with Qur'an, the Book of the Muslims and with Islamic life. So it's hard.

Most Christians I'm sure, if they're here in the audience, say, "This man has some nerve. How did he get the nerve that he is going to speak for us and say that African-Americans are going to favor his religion over our traditional religion?" But let us look at the two communities of Blacks, of African people or people of African descent and look at the Muslim – the African in Africa – who converted to the religion of Al-Islam. And then let us look at the descendant of African-Americans who was introduced to Christianity because of circumstances in America. In other words there was a Christian environment here and that was just a circumstance, so he became a Christian. Now let us look at the content of religion in the two lives, and look at the religious trends in the two lives. In the African people who have accepted the religion of Al-Islam we find that today, the African is still adhering to the idea of Al-Islam that was introduced to his people for five centuries, eight centuries, or even fourteen centuries ago. But look at the Black Christian masses in this country, and we find that they have lost a lot of the original content of Christianity or church life. That is a fact!

So we find that church life is weakening for the American Black, while Islamic life grows stronger in the African Black. And it's simply because Christianity has been hurt as being something that has appeal for Blacks. It has been hurt by White domination. And when I say White domination, I'm not talking about White rule, White political rule or White government rule. I'm not talking about that at all. When you pick up a Bible, you see White domination if it has pictures in it. And when you read about Christianity from books, an encyclopedia or religious books, you see White domination. Then when you look at the manifestation of God, you see White domination. I think all of this makes Christianity less appealing to free Blacks, and it makes Al-Islam more appealing. This is a difficulty in Christianity. But when you get down to the purity of a religion, we know then that we have the same God. However, the dress that they have given their theology and their religion makes it less acceptable to African-American people than Al-Islam.

WHITE DOMINATION IN CHRISTIANITY

IMH: Is that because of the imagery that you were speaking about?

WDM: Yes, it's just too much given in White pictures. And when you want to see something, it turns White. Now Muslims love the morals. White is also a symbol of moral substance, but this is not the problem. But when you take White, and make it as a symbol of God and say His Son is a White man, then God forbids us the Muslim to subscribe to such. The Muslim cannot accept for you to say His son is a White man or a Jew that's White too – for some people say, "well he's really not White, he's a Jew." And if you ask a Jew what race he belongs to, the Black or the White race, he says the White. Jews are identified as White people, too.

So that problem really exists there, and really it hurts White people too. Eventually we're going to find more White Christians doing what some Christians have done. In fact, there's a denomination of Christianity I have learned that have never imaged God. They have never done that. And those branches of Christianity that see Jesus as the Word of God and don't make any issue of his skin color or his ethnic origin or racial origin will still have a kind of equal footing with us as Muslims, when it comes to inviting Blacks or African-American people to a religion.

Again, however, we just mentioned the family. We mentioned the role that is given to family, to wife, to mother, and to father in our religion. We find that the African-American man has not been able to establish his family life. And I'm not talking about those few exceptions. I'm talking about the general rule. The general rule in America is that Black African-Americans are not established. In fact, when we had primitive sensitivities, when we were just released from slavery, we had a better sense of family as a majority, on the whole, than we have right now. There is neglect in the big cities in how we neglect our children, how we let gangs lead them, how we let them go into narcotics and into dope traffic, and how we let them abuse their precious lives. There is neglect in the family. There is neglect in how we don't even uphold Christian principles, if we're Christians in the home life. Too many of us have accepted to live on welfare and just because good jobs are not available is not an excuse. What's wrong with selling newspapers like many of our courageous and ambitious men are doing; they're going to sell newspapers rather than just accept idleness in their lives. We don't have that kind of demonstration of courage for the dignity of the person or for the dignity of the family. And I don't think it says too much for Christian society or Christian culture.

This is a terrible state of affairs. And I believe when African-American individuals or the families learn more about our religion, they are going to see that our religion is more "demanding" when it comes to family responsibility and the "male dignity in society." And strong African-American people want something more demanding. They don't want something that says you can just relax, lay down and die, or stay at home and nurse that adult size baby bottle and wait for the welfare check. We don't want that. We don't want to make our men soft and unprepared for the challenge of the world and challenge of life in the world. And I think that Christianity in a way is a little bit too compromising. It's a little bit too soft for the male needs in the African-American community.

Now that's not to put down a Christian. I believe that if a Christian will go back and search the Bible, search the New Testament for the message of strength, then they can help us. And that's what I hope the church will do. I hope the African-American Black church will go back and search the Gospel and the Old Testament, look in Proverbs, etc., for the message of strength and responsibility and preach that. But if they don't, then I'm going to still keep preaching that the Black African-American ought to choose my religion. Because we don't want to see this condition continue.

UNNATURAL GUILT OF THE WHITE SOCIETY

RI: Why do you think that the establishment fears that the African-American will come into Al-Islam?

WDM: For many reasons. And the main one is that there is still a lot of guilt in the Caucasian man, in the White society. They still feel that if African-American people got themselves in a situation of authority or power, that they might not be able to live with the scars of the past, the wrong-doings on a part of White America. Caucasians still fear that African-Americans may try to get even. That soreness may take its toll, and they might use their influence to get even with the White man. I know that there's a lot of fear of us "being able to have power and not seek revenge" or "not seek to punish" the White man, if we were put in a position of superiority, like he has punished us. The Caucasian punished us, when he had the power or when the country was more uncivilized.

However they should look at this. There are Blacks in Chicago, in Pittsburgh and other places who have realized a sense of authority and some degree of power. For example, we have Wendy's Fast Foods in Chicago on the Southside, and it is a franchise owned by a Black African-American. It's in a predominantly Black neighborhood; in fact, there are hardly any Whites living there. But they have a White Caucasian employed there. I think now they have at least two Whites employed, and they treat their employees, including their White employees, very nice. I know they do, because I go there and I don't see the White employees looking like they're uptight or looking like they're crying. They are just as relaxed and take care of business for the Black-owned fast food service operation.

Maybe you can remember back there in the sixties how a lot of the Blacks and the Whites were talking about the problem of the "Negro phobias." They are guilt-ridden, fearful, and unnaturally. That's partly due to the primitive sytle of human life, but greatly due to feelings of guilt. I am speaking about a certain class or a certain mentality of the White race. That is not speaking for the whole White race. I also think what is happening is that many of the other Whites have not yet confronted that situation consciously. They have not yet said, "Well, let me think about this rationally. Is there any proof that Black people are really seeking power, so they can turn the tables and get even with Whites for what their fathers suffered in this country?" If they would really give it some rational thought, they would say, "Oh hell, we're silly to be burdened with these ideas, with these fears. So let us look at the Blacks; their own movement in the mainstream of America proves that they have no desire to punish anybody!"

See, here's the thing I believe. That human beings can forgive anything. God has made us that way. We can forgive anything! All you have to do is just show us that the situation has changed. That the circumstances have changed and their hearts have changed, and that it is a new day. African-American Blacks will have to be aware, too, that they have to understand what America has really done. It has done a great job, because afterall, Whites are the majority; Whites do hold the power. Especially in the South, we should understand this. I think the South should be commended for the ability to just transform in terms of their attitude towards African-American Blacks. They have been able to transform the South in a matter of twenty years. Now they have Black mayors, Black governors, and Black people are represented in government.

Look at the business and progress there in Atlanta where the Blacks and the Whites are all working together to make that a reality. The South has to be commended, and Blacks ought to see that. I'm not saying we ought to close our eyes to the problems that we're still facing as Blacks. No, don't close our eyes. But don't close your eyes, too, to the great changes that have been brought about in this country, because of White support to Black people not accepting to be mistreated or not accepting that injustice be the order of the day in America.

So there's a lot of healing that's needed. And the healing that's needed on the part of Black suffering and the White man's fears and guilt feelings will take moral courage. It will take courage to say, "I'm going to look at the facts, and I'm going to open my eyes." When a person closes their eyes to the realities of the day, they don't know that in doing that is really a strain also. This is really a burden, too. It's a burden on me to close my eyes. That's a serious burden. I have to look out on the world and see a White man that's accepting Blacks and who is being fair to his employees and not discriminating against Blacks. And because I'm still experiencing some difficulty as a Black person in America, I don't want to see him so that I pass a White man like that. I close my eyes and don't want to look at him.

There is also the White who has realized some sense of comfort and security in the White man's competitive society by imposing upon themselves a belief that Blacks are inferior, when they walk by the Black mayor who's successfully leading the city and talking care of the affairs of his office like mayor Maynard Jackson was doing in Atlanta, and like the mayor who's doing it right now, like the mayor in Chicago is doing – both of them are doing wonderful jobs given the circumstances and the problems that they have to face. They have to close their eyes to that; they don't want to see those Blacks. They don't want to see what they are doing. So really we're torturing ourselves, and we're burdening ourselves unnecessarily.

Personally, I have no desire to be a White man. I'm speaking for myself. I mean, there are some Blacks that want to be White, but I don't want to be White. I admire the Caucasian White man. God made him, and that's his makeup. God didn't make me White. God made me African-American. And I have no desire to be White; I have no desire to have White children. I have no desire to live in a White neighborhood. I just have the desire to live in a good neighborhood. And I think poor Whites and poor Blacks are victims of people who exploit the weaknesses of the poor Whites and the poor Blacks, people who set up something to capitalize from. And the poor Blacks and the poor Whites will find themselves in a situation, and they will say, "Oh, the Blacks won't live with themselves, the Black just want to move in our neighborhoods!" In Chicago we have a big problem like that. The Whites say "the Blacks can't manage their own communities. They can't keep decent stores, they can't keep decent housing and decent neighborhoods, and they run away from their own problems and run into our neighborhoods." Whites have these complaints. We have to respect something in their complaints. But it is also a very confused situation.

It is not something that they can charge to Blacks and hold it over the Black African-American. That's not the case. The problem is that Blacks have always come behind Whites since slavery. We have never come into something that was ours. Whatever we came into, Whites had it first. And there's a pattern, it seems, of only letting us in after they have gotten everything they possibly could out of that neighborhood or out of that situation. They let us in after financial problems have multiplied, maintenance of property problems have multiplied and become too burdensome, and many of these Whites then want to move out of these areas. These areas then have become unattractive to them or for them. That is the case.

Then when Blacks move in there with their small means, they find themselves with a heavier financial responsibility than the Whites had when they first moved into the area. Businesses have deteriorated. Housing has deteriorated. Public services have deteriorated to some degree before the Whites moved out. Then we come in there with smaller means and have to be expected to carry or shoulder that great burden. Now I don't say that we should charge that all to White folks. We shouldn't charge it all to White folks. It is partly our responsibility, because our established people, business people, civic people should have the foresight to look ahead and say, "Look, this is a situation that's going to be too taxing. We are multiplying, and some of us will have to move into White areas. But we have a responsibility also to recover what has been lost in this area." There is not enough effort in this respect. Pittsburgh does not have the same kind of problem that we have in Chicago. There is not the segregated pattern here that we find in Chicago. At least, I haven't seen it.

In Chicago, you can go for miles and miles in the Black neighborhood, and you will never see anything but a Black neighborhood. And there are other big cities in the United States like that where there are very obvious segregation patterns or racial patterns. Chicago has the Black Southside, the Black Westside, the White Westside, and the White Northside. We have that in Chicago, and in many other cities there is the same problem. And a lot of this racial hostility, racial antagonism, I believe, is coming from people who are blaming Blacks or are charging Blacks with abandoning Black communities and their responsibility to Black communities to bring their problems over into the White community. That's something that we should look at, and we need the help of our political leaders and our civic leaders, and our business leaders. We need their help to study this situation and direct the concerns of Blacks to this problem. Because it's very serious and we're not going to have the normalization of racial relations in this country, until we tackle that problem. I think this is a very serious concern.

THE EDUCATION OF THE WOMAN IS TO EDUCATE A NATION

RI: Imam Hassain, please comment.

IMH: Yes, I see in the Imam's answers here that it touches the cause of these great problems that exist. I think one of the major detriments that has gone on from the past up to now is that people aren't dealing with the causes of things. There was a saying one time that goes, "To educate a man would be to educate an individual. But to educate a woman, you educate a nation." That saying shows the great need for education of the woman. And what I see in what the Imam is saying is that women need proper education. And I believe the best source of that would be to return to Scripture.

WDM: I'm going to have to go along with you, although, I don't know if we are putting ourselves in a bad situation with the women or not. But I'm going to have to go along with you, and it's the second time you have mentioned the woman's role in this. I agree that a man's nature is to support his woman, when it comes to housing needs or home needs. And I do believe that our women sometimes put too much demands on their man. Our women are going to have to learn that until we can recover, they're going to have to lessen their demands on their husbands.

You know every woman is born a queen, and every woman wants a castle. All right, but wait until I'm able to get it. Have patience with me, until I'm able to get it. And don't demand more material comforts in your life, than you know your husband can manage. But have patience with him. We have to understand that what we see on television is "America," and what we are is "African-American." So when we see Caucasian White folks on television with castles and things, and Blacks with their one-hundred-thousand dollar homes or two-hundred-fifty-thousand dollar homes, two or three fine cars, the wife of that man who's earning one-hundred-fifty dollars a week or two- or three-hundred dollars a week is going to have to understand that her husband is not that fella she's looking at on the television. And she is not the wife of that fella that she's looking at on the the television. Their situation and their cirucmstances are drastically different from what she's looking at on television. We're going to have to look at America without losing our reality in America.

The woman has to have patience with her man. And I think many times the man will move out of the area, and many men want to do something with the properties they have. He will say, "Look, I think I can whip this property into shape and remodel this room, put some paint on here, spend a few dollars and improve upon the property we have." But the woman says, "Look, you've got a good job now. We can afford to move into that other neighborhood. I want something else." So many times it is the woman's fault.

TAKE CARE OF OUR NEEDS FIRST

IMH: So we've come to the point, I believe, that as we reach the cause of thing, we have to sometimes accept the fact that we have to address our needs instead of just what we want. I think that's a big thing in the lives of people now.

WDM: If we don't start giving some respect to what we need, so that we want what we need, rather than concentrating on what we can't get, I'm telling you, we will just be undermining the little accomplishments that we have made as people in this country and as Americans. Because you can't keep spending "plastic money." Plastic money runs out eventually. People take the plastic tokens back, and then you find yourself in jail or desperate again. So we have to stop somewhere.

RI: That's right.

IMH: Imam Muhammad, do you see Al-Islam in the time we've had the privilege to practice this religion over the last forty to fifty years bringing the African-American to that point?

WDM: I most certainly do. And I invite the Urban League or any of these groups that study trends in the African-American community conditions to study the Muslim population of America. And they'll find that we are making progress materially as well as spiritually.

PROGRESS IS THE RESPONSIBILITY OF THE INDIVIDUAL

RI: Imam Muhammad, recently you made an address that said that the best way to make progress in this country is to have an individual to carry the greatest amount of responsibility for his own individual life. Do you feel that is the problem in the African-Americans' lives, being that we carry the least amount of responsibility?

WDM: Yes, and it's very obvious that the African-American community carries the least amount of responsibility of ethnic members of an American society for the state of their community. For example, in Chicago we know that the African-American contribution to the tax base is hardly present at all, and it's because we're the poorest in establishment. When I say in establishment, I'm not only talking about business, although that's the first one we look at – how we're established in business, when we compare our involvement in business with the involvement of the other native Americans. We are hardly represented. Most of the thriving business streets in the heart of the African-American neighborhood or community in Chicago are either owned by non-African-Americans or supported by non-African-Americans. Very few real good businesses or strong businesses are carried by the African-American. However, that's just part of the establishment that we're talking about." We're also talking about our contribution to cultural establishment. How much are we contributing to clean art forms. At one time we were very popular for blues and jazz, and we had intellectual movements and cultural movements to some extent represented in men like Benjamin Mays and others, who are figures for the African-American focus. But as time has passed, we're losing those personalities who, themselves, privately conducted a struggle for establishing the African-American as an intellectual and for establishing the African-American as a citizen with sensitive cultural concerns. All of that now seems to be kind of diminishing. And the family life of the African-American, which was in a poor condition materially, perhaps is better off now, as far as the amount of money we have to spend. But in the past we were better off on the whole as a race, than we have been in this country, in spite of economic problems and unemployment problems. But the creativity of the African-American has not improved and has not increased. The African-American as a productive citizen has not increased. There's just more money available because of a society that has become more consumer-oriented. And therefore it is expected that any citizen of the United States must have spending money. In some kind of way, we do get spending money, but we are not established. When you look at the home institution, we are not as established as families as we used to be. We used to have stronger African-American families.

THE MUSLIM'S BEHAVIOR SHOULD CONFORM TO AL-ISLAM

RI: How does the religion of Al-Islam require that the African-Americans, the new converts in the religion, make changes in their life?

WDM: There's heavy emphasis on the family responsibility and to one's family in our religion. Any person who takes his religion very seriously, I would say a church person who takes his religion very seriously, will have a more disciplined family. If a businessman or businesswoman are in business, they will take that business very serious. Then that business involvement, that business devotion, is going to have some affect on the discipline of that family. But most of our families live just like the character of American families. Most of the families are not really deeply involved in anything like a business development or religious devotion to that extent, that you make your own behavior conform to your religious principles. Most of us think it is enough just to say, "I go to church." We don't devote ourselves to the extent that we make our behavior conform to our religious principles. Whereas in Al-Islam, if a Muslim's behavior doesn't conform to his religious principles, his behavior is frowned upon by Muslims. Even in our community we have new converts to this religion. If we see a Muslim conducting himself in an unIslamic way, we don't like that. And we may even call attention to him in the public. "Brother, you shouldn't be behaving like that, if you're a Muslim."

The male in the Muslim family leads the prayers. So to pray in our religion, even though it's not at home or is not private, if more than one person is involved, one has to take a position of leader. We can pray alone or in private prayer which is the sunnah of the Prophet. But we also have to pray, which is more important, in a group as a family. And the greatest demonstration of that is our congregational prayer at the mosque or at any gathering where we all come together to pray. In any situation, whether it's public or a mosque, if it involves more than one person, there must be a leader. So the religion automatically makes a leader in the family. There is a family head or the elder in the family. The elder in the family becomes a leader. In most cases it's the father. And I think that's very important for a family, especially for a Muslim family, to have recognition from the family to an elder or to a member that deserves that recognition. And our religion supports that.

RI: Yes. I remember when we were growing up at home, that our mother and father would make the eldest child responsible for the rest of us.

ARRIVAL INTO THE INTERNATIONAL MUSLIM COMMUNITY

RI: Imam, you recently asked us to drop the name, American Muslim Mission. Could you explain why?

WDM: Yes. It's just the final step in the process of bringing our membership into the international Muslim community and to conform to where there's a normal Islamic life – just normal, practical, Islamic life. The hangover from yesterday of "Black nationalist" influence is something that we have to get rid of, because it was in conflict with the open society and democratic order of an Islamic community.

APATHETIC FEELINGS IN AFRICAN-AMERICAN PEOPLE FOR A REPUBLICAN ADMINISTRATION

RI: Brother Imam, there seems to be a sense of apathy in the African-American community, since the re-election of President Reagan. Do you think that our feelings are correct or are they incorrect?

WDM: They are correct and incorrect at the same time. There is not as much human-based sentimentalism during the Republican administration. You can hear more talk and more sentiments expressed for all-around human beings and humanity. But we are even hearing less of that now. That's good in a sense, in my opinion. But then again, it's not so good. We don't want to lose the genuine concern for a human being, for a life, for the health of a human being, for opportunities of all human beings, and those humanitarian feelings in society. We don't want to lose that. But I do think that under the Democrats, after the Korean War and the evils that came out of that war, those experiences made people turn and take on a kind of extreme from one of cruelty towards man and then to a kind of romanticism or overly sentimental attitude towards man as a human being and humanity as such. I think the coming of the Republicans into office has had an affect of bringing us from that extreme to approach the problems of man in a more rational way and in a more practical way. For some this has meant the loss of interest in the human being and the human person and in the promotion of humanity. But I would say, on the whole, the Reagan administration has been good for the country.

THE LACK OF CONTROL IN AFRICAN-AMERICAN LIVES CAUSES DESTRUCTION

RI: Imam, last year there were 6,165 African-Americans that were murder victims; 5,847 of them or 95 percent of the offenders were African-Americans. Now that's very alarming. How can we as an ethnic group help to stop this?

WDM: It's a pity. It's a pity that we have this situation in our racial group. I think it's a problem that has developed because of lack of faith in ourselves, repeated disappointments, putting up too much hope and expectations that perhaps were a little bit too unrealistic. We're not realistic enough. We have been a kind of people from slavery who have moved from one condition of dependency to another condition of dependency, even though we're free. Now, what I'm referring to is the movement from the plantation or from the slave master to a dependency on the Democratic party for bread or for advancement in this country. We expect the President of the United States to be a parent to us.

The President of the United States may be to the Jew just the President of the United States. Maybe the Jew won't even be interested, except for certain political needs outside of the country because of Israel being established in the Middle East. The same thing for the Irish and others. They will not be so heavily dependent upon one man in the government of America – the President of these United States, or upon one part of the Democratic party as we are today. So we have come from a state of heavy dependency, looking to the slave master when we were slaves for our future and to take care of our welfare, and then coming out of that to depend upon social programs so heavily and the Democratic party so heavily to look out for our future, to promise us jobs, to guarantee us a good tomorrow. So that amount of extreme help that we have demanded because of past experience is not our nature.

We have exceptions in our race. We have Black men and women that go forward, and they're not dependent. They hardly know what's happening in Washington, because they're busy creating things and making things work for them and work for the country – building business and advancing themselves. But that's the rare exception. Most of us look to somebody to lead us – a minister of the church, or a minister in religion to lead us. And the minister has to guarantee us that he has some kind of direct line to the President or to somebody in the government, in the Democratic party or whatever.

That heavy dependency is responsible for our abuse of each other. Because when people are so heavily dependent like that, abnormally dependent upon forces and circumstances outside of their community, then it creates a state or situation of hopelessness, of despair, of depression. And because they don't have in themselves a sense of security, a sense of command, a sense of where they're going, a feeling that they are making tomorrow for themselves, when people live in a state like that, then their energies will be vented destructively. And who is the most likely prey? It is the one nearest to them. So we take it out on each other. And that's responsible for this high homocide rate. It's not that we are criminals. We are not criminals. But our productive energies have not found opportunity yet under our own supervision.

RI: I guess having the lack of control over our lives turns inwards on ourselves.

WDM: Yes, it turns against Blacks. It turns inwards, exactly.

THE DESPERATION OF AFRICAN-AMERICAN RELIGIOUS LEADERSHIP

RI: Imam, when you're speaking about how we look to a minister to have direct contact with a congressman or the President or someone, do you feel that our religious leadership in the African-American community is helping us or is it hurting us in this situation?

WDM: I believe in most cases now the religious leadership, in the average African-American neighborhood or community, is negatively affecting us. And I believe that because most of the leaders in the African-American community are really desperate people, men that are desperate or sense a desperate need to survive themselves. They sense a desperate need to survive, not monetarily, not dollar-wise, for I'm not talking about that, although that's there too. But there is a desperate need to survive as a leader with appeal to their members. And most of them are not as orientated religiously as they used to be when I was a boy. They are not as orientated religiously. They don't even speak with religious concern that most ministers spoke with when I was a boy. I used to listen to a Christian program on the radio, and I've even visited Christian churches. Today, they try to stay current. And the mistake of most of the religious leaders is that they want to stay current. So whatever is the big issue now — they try to address that big issue. And they have let the human life just slip away from them.

IMH: Imam, would you think that Muslim modern-day ministers know these thing to be a fact?

WDM: Sure, I know they do, because many of them, as you know, are very educated. They are very intelligent men; they are well educated; they are well informed. But I think they're afraid to be different. I'm sure many of them are aware of their own neglect. But I think they feel that to be different is to risk the scorn of their associates. And more than anything, religion requires that you stand up for what is right, no matter what the consequences may be.

IMH: Yes, probably they are just going the way they think their people want them to go, instead of taking a stand on their independency and leadership.

WDM: Certainly. And I think that's their desperation again, that desperation in the African-American community. Even our ministers are affected by that desperation, because they don't have a grip on their lives, and they probably don't have control of the destiny of their communities, not as much control on the destiny of their communities as Irish or Italians or these new Asians that are coming in may have. So I think this desperation is expressing itself, too, even where the ministers are concerned. And maybe they are not aware of that. But they, too, have a spirituality that is weakened and confused because of them not coming to grips with their own responsibility as members of this society or members of their neighborhood.

THE ECONOMIC STATE OF AFRICAN-AMERICANS

RI: Yes sir. Imam, could you give us your view of the economic state of the African-American today?

WDM: The economic state of the African-American today, in my opinion, is hardly any better. In fact, I think it is worse than it was fifty years ago. We have more numbers now. Today we might number 25 million to 30 million people. Fifty years ago the number was much smaller. So we will see a greater presence of African-Americans in business. But if a study is made, and some studies have been made, we will see from the study that the African-American today is not as economically established or established business-wise as he was, say, twenty-five or thirty years ago. Too many of us now are afraid to invest, and too many of us invest for just weekend thrills. So we can't establish ourselves. A couple of generations back most of us invested because we wanted a better image as a person, a better image as a family member, or a better image as a person belonging to that neighborhood. We wanted to establish a credit for ourselves. And many of us invested because we wanted to see our children have a better chance than we had. But that is non-existent in the African-American community as it was in those days. I think it's growing and is coming back because of economic realities, but it is not coming back fast enough.

THE MORAL STATE WILL DETERMINE
THE ECONOMIC STATE FOR AFRICAN-AMERICANS

RI: Brother Imam, do you think that the economic state would be much more secure or could develop much better, if our moral state in the African-American community was better developed?

WDM: Yes. God points out to us in our Holy Book a place or vicinity that really offered hardly any opportunity at all for material advancement. And that is where the Kaa'ba, the holy center for Muslims in Arabia is located. It is in the sandy deserts of Saudi Arabia. But out there in that barren land, the Arab tribes have always been able to survive, and they're known for being men of trade or men of commerce. It is because they have a business ethic. God has blessed them through Muhammad to keep a business ethic, to keep a sense of business and community purity. That area the sacred area around the house where we turn when we pray, the Qiblah for Muslims or the direction for Muslims when we pray, even before Prophet Muhammad was mission by God, peace and blessings be on him, was a place that was looked upon as a restricted place. The Arabs just couldn't behave any kind of way there.

You know, many shameful practices had come in, because of deviation from the Word of Abraham, and the Prophet had to bring religion back from that confusion and corruption. But, even during that time of ignorance and corruption, they had respect for that precinct, for that home or for that sacred precinct, and they forced themselves to behave differently when they were in that area. Because of them having respect for something above them, something higher than man, something bigger than man, even though they believed in false gods and they had bad idols in their religion which was rejected by God, but because of that respect they had a better opportunity and a better situation for themselves materially and business-wise.

They were men of trade. They were men of commerce. They bartered with each other. They would go outside of the precincts. They would travel to Syria. They would travel to many countries and they would bring goods back, and they would sell them there. And they would carry the few things, the commodities that they could produce and they would sell them elsewhere. So it has always been a commercial-based community or a business community. It is because of the focus on family life, respect for family life, respect for a finer life that the Quraysh as a noble tribe had, even before Prophet Muhammad, and respect for its members was great. So God is the factor there. God is the factor there for bringing that about, even though they confused their idea of God before the coming of the Prophet, peace and blessing be upon him. And most of all, there is a belief that you shouldn't be dishonest in business. If we would have a higher level of that kind of conscienceness in the African-American business community, we would find better business. Yes, a moral base is absolutely necessary for a real sustained business growth.

RI: Well, Imam Muhammad, we have enjoyed our interview with you, and we're very thankful to have you here today. And I know Imam Hassain feels the same as I do. We have about a half a minute, and I'd like to let everyone know that we've had the opportunity to have an interview with Imam W. Deen Muhammad from Chicago, and my co-host Imam Mustafa Hassain. I'd like to give you the greetings, As-Salaamu-Alaikum.

PART V

January 19, 1987

It is Allah Who is responsible for the existence of everything; He's responsible for the design in the creation and the potential in me. We should seek to realize our potential and to perform the excellence that we are able to perform within society and through society. But don't have society as the last hope for that. Allah is the hope for that and is the aim in our life — to plese Him and to meet the demands He has placed on us. "That is why America is so great, for many of the Founding Fathers were inspired with that kind of idea."

Imam W. Deen Mohammed

ان الله هو الذي خلق كل شيءالله هو الذي انشأنا إنشأ مانحن فيه . وعلينا ان نبحث على افضل طريقه نخدم بها انفسنا ونخدم المجتمع لا ان نخدم المجتمع في سبيل المجتمع بل علينا ان نخدم المجتمع في سبيل الله والله هو غايتنا . علينا ان نقوم بما يرضى الله تعالى .

RI: As-Salaamu-Alaikum. Ladies and gentlemen, we're glad to be in your home once again. The title of our program is "Al-Islam in Focus." We have a rare privilege of having Imam W. Deen Muhammad here, and our co-host, Imam Mustafa Hassain. So I'd like to give the greetings to both Imams — As-Salaamu-Alaikum.

WDM
& Wa-Alaikum As-Salaam.
IMH

AL—ISLAM TRUE FREEDOM FOR AMERICAN MUSLIMS

RI: We are going through a series of programs with our leader, Imam Muhammad, and we're giving a view from the Islamic perspective. So, I'd like to begin by first asking Imam Muhammad this question. Recently we have heard that you have dissolved the American Muslim Mission, and more recently you have resigned as the Imam of the Chicago Masjid. Would you explain to us why you have made these decisions?

WDM: Yes. The idea that the American Muslim as a community has been dissolved is incorrect. What was dissolved was the old organizational structure that we inherited from the past. It was not suitable for propagating the religion as the religion is given in the Holy Book, the Qur'an. So the military aspect of the old community is behind us, and the centralization of all business activities and the hiring of people or employing people or recruiting people all over the country is all finished. That's left up to individuals. The centralization even of the ministry that resembled a kind of priesthood before is all done away with. But to say that the American Muslim community has been dissolved is incorrect. That gives the impression that there is no more interest in propagating the religion — that's incorrect.

To the contrary, there's more activity now, because people are freer locally to do things and to carry their responsibility as Muslims. And the individuals are freer to use their own talents or individual talents and make progress for themselves. This way is more Islamic now. Before it was more of a kind of social reform organization, or a militant organization for social reform in the name of religion. And a big majority of the members back then, I believe, were religious people but the outer image was incorrect. So we have not done away with the community and the commitment to be Muslims and to prosper in America as Muslims, to work together and cooperate with each other – we haven't done away with that at all.

Now to address the second question. I resigned the position of Resident Imam in Chicago to free myself from what I feel was something that limited my own ability to serve the religion. I feel more comfortable with a responsibility to all of the Muslims of America, and not to any *particular* Muslims in America. And I feel more comfortable being free from a lot of organization. I think religion can become too organized that the organization begins to defeat the purpose.

IMAM W. DEEN MUHAMMAD — APPOINTED TO SUPREME COUNCIL OF MASAJID

RI: Imam, on that same line, the appointment to the Supreme Council of Masajid for you that was recently announced, tell us about that.

WDM: It is a Council of Mosques; mosques are our religious places of worship. The Council only serves as a supportive body to assist and lend its resources to the Masjid or Mosque. And to the Imams and to the mosque leaders for the improvement of Islamic knowledge and for the improvement of Islamic propagation or the spreading of that knowledge to others. It is for better Islamic schools, if they have schools. This Council is based in Saudi Arabia, but the members are located all over the world. And I have been appointed to a position on that Council for the American Mosques or the masajid in America. The word masjid is Arabic; the word "mosque" is the term used in America. I have not yet started my term. My term perhaps will start in November, and I have not had the opportunity to even meet with persons who head that organization. In November, God willing, I will meet with them, and then I will know what my role is going to be. Right now, I'm somewhat in the dark.

IMAM MUHAMMAD — THE FIRST AFRICAN-AMERICAN APPOINTED TO SUPREME COUNCIL OF MOSQUES

RI: Another question on that line, how significant is that in the sense of an African-American being appointed to that position?

WDM: As I see it, it is very significant. African-Americans have not only an African past, but we also have an Islamic past. Fifty percent of Africa belongs to a religion we call "Islam," and even before we were brought as slaves to America or willingly came to America, there were many Muslims in Africa. And the likelihood of some of us having ancestors in the past who were Muslims is very, very, very much a possibility. And not only is this documented elsewhere that some of the slaves who were brought over were Muslims – that is also documented right here in America. So it is very, very significant that after all of those generations and now three centuries or more the religion has become known in the African-American community, and a son of a poor black man from Georgia is now associated Muslims and bodies of Muslim nations all over the world and has been appointed to a Supreme Council that is based in Saudi Arabia where the holy precincts of Mecca are. We know the cities of our Prophet, peace be upon him, are all in Saudi Arabia. So I think it's very, very significant.

THE HONORABLE ELIJAH MUHAMMAD HELPED RAISE THE AFRICAN-AMERICAN FROM DUST TO INDUSTRY

RI: Do you feel that history will ever accurately record the social progress that your father, the late Honorable Elijah Muhammad, made for the African-American?

WDM: I hope so. But that responsibility falls on us first. We knew him best. So I hope that some of our scholarly people who really *knew* the Honorable Elijah Muhammad will accept the responsibility for preserving his really great contributions in the role of social reform and moral uplifting, and in his trying to inspire industry from the poor people who neglected themselves and were neglected by society for so long. I hope that they will appreciate that and do a scholarly job of preserving that in history.

THE RESURGENCE OF THE ISLAMIC LIFE THROUGHOUT THE WORLD

RI: Imam Muhammad, currently we see an upheaval going on in Islamic countries, and they're trying to get back to the true Islamic governments. Do you feel that there's a resurgence of the Islamic mind or thinking going on throughout the world now?

WDM: Certainly it is. It's throughout the world, and I'm glad you asked the question and put it that way. It's not just Iran. You know of it mostly because of the political problems that our nation or our government has with Iran and the kind of zealot activities that we associate with the Iranian movement. The recent Iranian movement in Al-Islam makes us think that that's where the activity is, but that is not correct. It is all over – in Africa, in Asia, Pakistan, even in India where there is a great Muslim community numbering in better than 80 million or more Muslims. All over we are seeing this resurgence.

In America we have seen a big organization that was very significant in the 60's. I believe it was Readers Digest that published on its cover page that the most significant Black man at that time was Elijah Muhammad, who headed that body of people who called themselves Muslims under the name of "Black Muslims" in the Press. But that movement has converted to the religion that's attained by one billion Muslims throughout the world. I think that shows that if there is not a resurgence then there is certainly a whole lot of activity in at least a segment of the African-American or the Black community in this country. Another thing is that it is not fanatical. For the most part it is far from being fanatical.

It's a curiosity in the international world. And what I mean by that is among the nations of Muslims there is this new interest in the religion. This is because they realize now a freedom that they didn't realize for perhaps some 10 years, 30 years, and for most of them even 50 years or 100 years. Before now they hadn't realized an independence from colonialism. You know, in the late 40s and in the 50s a lot of the Muslim nations had just gotten their freedom from colonial domination. So we are now seeing Muslims getting interested in their religion with more freedom and more independence than they ever have enjoyed since the colonial occupations of those nations.

So Americans should understand that this curiosity in Al-Islam, this resurgence is not all coming from a fanatical or zealot kind of situation. It is not that at all. Most of it is just an intellectual curiosity and a purely religious curiosity. And we are serving people who are just hungry to know something about their own religion that was kept from them during the days of colonial occupation. Many western powers were able to take over the teaching of the religion in Muslim countries.

AL-ISLAM SATISFIES THE NATURE IN MAN

RI: You know, I have quite a few friends at work who, like you said, out of intellectual curiosity had begun studying the religion and have found out how close it is to their nature and want to know more and more about it.

WDM: Yes. This is true for any legitimate religion. That is if a religion has come purely into existence through innocent, God-fearing upright people, that religion satisfies something in the nature of man. God created us, and God created our nature. So anything that God inspires is going to satisfy something in the nature of man. And as you know, for Muslims our religion redeems nature in man's estimation. It is man's estimation that sometimes sees nature as something beneath him something degrading, and he tries to take on an angel nature or a god nature. We believe that kind of achievement is impossible for man. Man can only be man; he can't be God. So our religion has redeemed nature in our own estimation and in our own mind's eye. And it places very much importance on respect for the goal of nature, and the goal of nature is excellence.

AL-ISLAM FOCUSES ON THE LIFE OF THE INDIVIDUAL

RI: Could you explain how the religion acts in the life of the individual? What role does it play in the life of an individual?

WDM: Yes. Like democracy in America, our religion focuses on the individual as the best safeguard. If we build up the individual, give him proper understanding of his religion, make it possible for him to get a correct Islamic understanding, or get correct informtion, then that's the best way of establishing or propagating or representing a religion. Concentrate on the individual. The religion has this in itself, in its Holy Source the Qur'an which is the best source and the most authentic source, because it is perfect for us. In the life of the Prophet, in the traditions of our Prophet Muhammad, which is second to the Qur'an as the authentic source for Muslims as well as in the Qur'an the focus is on the individual; it makes its appeal mostly to the individual.

The Qur'an is not a Book to call nations to a mission; it's a Book that calls individuals to life, and it gives the individual a daily program for assuring that individual that he'll have a good life and a full life, if he follows that daily program. He's reminded daily by daily prayers that can't just be said when he feels like it. He'd be neglecting the disciplines of that religion, if he says his prayers just when he feels like it. He has to say them on time. God says in our Holy Book that prayers have been prescribed for stated times, for regulated times, and we know we pray regularly five times a day at specific times. A Muslim can't just eat anything he wants. Muslims have a Muslim diet. He can't just go to bed just as he feels like going to bed; he's suppose to go to bed with the Name of God and knowing that God gives life and God gives death. God is over life and God is over death. He can't arise just as he feels he should arise. He must arise knowing that he has to make his ablution, clean himself up, make his Adhan or hear the Adhan, and respond to the call of God and go make his prayers first thing in the day – the very *first* thing in the day.

So a Muslim's whole life is regulated on a daily basis. Every day is regulated. And there are so many other requirements in the life of Muslims. Some people say "Oh, I don't want that much discipline — I don't want that much burden in my life." Well, if they don't, then the Muslim religion is not for them. This religion is for people who love to give their whole life to God. And in so doing, God lets you have your whole life.

RI: Yes sir. So in other words, by giving your life to God, God blesses you with having control over your life.

WDM: Certainly.

IMH: Brother Imam, first of all I want to let you know we certainly appreciate you taking your time out of your busy schedule to come here to Pittsburgh.

WDM: This is my business. I don't call this taking time out. When I get an opportunity to be a spokesman for what is right or for my religion, that's my business.

IMH: Then that brings me to the question I want to ask you, or a comment I want to make about your resignation as Imam from the Chicago Masjid. It gives you a more universal freedom to get about and explain these things like you're doing. And in the way you put it, that religion should fit an individual like a good suit of clothes – he shouldn't be tightened up. In other words, he should be comfortable with the religion. And in studying the life of Prophet Muhammad, peace and blessings be upon him, he stressed that he was just a normal, natural man.

WDM: Yes he did.

IMH; And by having the religion pointed out as you're doing concerning the individual, I've been following your writings in the Muslim Journal on the success of the individual, and it makes one feel that he doesn't have to have a group of people before his religion benefits him. It benefits him as an individual. So, do you feel that your resignation as Resident Imam in Chicago takes you away from the problems of people?

WDM: Yes. That type of situation is taxing. To meet people, to serve a small congregation if you're cut out more for a kind of evangelistic role, though that is a Christian term, then I think you hurt yourself by staying in one place all the time and letting your energies be tied up by one small congregation. Not that I didn't like that. I got great satisfaction from serving the Masjid or the Mosque in Chicago. There was great satisfaction. In fact, as you know, I have gotten my growth and development right there in Chicago.

THE FAMILY STRUCTURE IN AL-ISLAM

RI: Imam, could you explain how the role of religion and how it should come to play in the life of the family structure?

WDM: In the family structure of Muslims the mother and father as authorities is very, very important. We believe that the woman has been created by God to be our first teacher, and that the teachings that most children get are from a responsible mother. She gives encouragement for good behavior, for respect for authority, respect for adults. She gives awareness of things in the world that are harmful and things that are good, and that you should shun those things that are harmful, that are crimes, that are the life of a drunkard, that are dope, and all of these things. The alert mother is naturally sensitive to her responsibility, and she works to groom her child, to raise her child, and prepare her child so when that child goes out from her supervision that child will make it most likely in the world without becoming a victim of those things that are very harmful or criminal.

So this education is a good common sense education. We believe that the first foundation of common sense comes from mother, whether she's educated or not. God has prepared her and has created her with the sensitivities and everything to give us that first foundation. So in the Muslim home the man stands back, and he waits for the wife to involve him. If she doesn't ask him to come help with her children, he waits for her. He sees that as her supervision. That's the domain of her supervision – the home. But she sees him as her husband and as an authority in terms of where the money's going to come from, and how are we going to manage the bills. Also if "there's a problem here – my child has a problem in the streets. Some boys are threatening him." She goes to the husband and says, "the neighbors around are not the kind of neighbors we would like to raise our children around. I would like to move." Or she may feel, "This boy is getting too manly. He's getting too disrespectful, and I can't talk to him." Then she would go to the husband. But for the most part, the husband is kind of out of the picture; he's in the background. And the woman runs the house.

The informed Muslim husband won't say "Look, I want you to put wallpaper on these walls, not paint." The informed Muslim husband would never tell his wife that, unless he can't afford what she's asking for; then he'd say "Well, I can't afford this now. Let's get somethig else." That's different, you know. But he doesn't take over her house and insist that one room be pink and the other one be red or something like that. He sees that as her domain, and he doesn't interfere with her teaching and raising of the children. If he has some help for her, he will do it in privacy when the children are not around and can't hear what he's saying. So that is very important. Though the man takes that backseat kind of role in the matters of the house and in the rearing of the children, he's still obviously the boss. That is because God has required that he leads the prayers. So the mother will tell the children, "It's time for prayer, get ready." And if the father's there, she says, "Your father's going to lead you in prayer." Every Muslim father, every Muslim husband should accept that responsibility that he has to lead his family in the religion, that he has to lead them in prayer. Not that he's going to be teaching them what the Qur'an says for children and so on. She does all that; she is a teacher. But when it comes to leading them in prayer, he's supposed to be their leader. And if he leads them in prayer, then he establishes that *he* believes in God, and that *he* is obedient to God. And that's very, very, very much important.

IMH: That helps, Brother Imam, for the children to be disciplined to the parents by the father showing that he has something that he believes in and that he's disciplined to.

WDM: Certainly. If the children see discipline and respect in you for authority above you, then that's going to help them recognize you in your position of authority. That's true. I agree.

MAN'S HIGHEST DEVELOPMENT IS FOLLOWING THE DISCIPLINE OF GOD

RI: So, the life of a Muslim is the life of discipline.

WDM: Certainly it is a life of discipline. In fact, we see our religion as really a higher expression of man and a higher expression of what God has done in the external world. These bodies that we have to exist upon, as with the earth, are fed by energies from the sun. And the moon is very important in the life of man, as is all of these bodies and all of these forces operating in the universe. They're under law also. They're disciplined. And we believe that the highest development of man is for him to conform to the universal discipline God intended for him – that's the *highest* development possible for man.

And again regarding prayer, there are the obligatory prayers and the sunnah prayers. And the family prays with the congregation, but they also have to pray alone. To pray alone in our religion means you have to know something about the Qur'an, because you have to recite Qur'an in our prayers. So you have to know some verses from Qur'an. Also you have to be able to go through every step in prayer. You have to know what the Ka'bah is; you have to be able to direct yourself towards the Ka'bah - the Holy House of Mecca built by Abraham the Prophet and his son, Ismael, peace be upon them.

So that's a sign right there, that in our religion the individual must be responsible for his religious life. If the individual is neglected, then we will just preach religion and give rituals and the individual is not given the opportunity to learn something from the men in this religion, to get some insights as he grows into adult age. A young man should grow also in the ability to perceive. There are even greater messages in his religion from the reading and study of the Holy Book, the Qur'an. He should be able to come into a town where there's no Muslims and practice his religious life and not have to go to the Mosque or to church, or any holy place to have someone remind him that he should be Muslim or that he should practice his religion. He should be able to where there's no other Muslim and still live his Muslim life and practice his religion. He should be able to conduct himself properly as a Muslim in business, properly as a citizen in the country, as a neighbor to his neighbor who is non-Muslim although he is Muslim; he should be able to do all of that by himself.

The true Muslim should even be able to establish a new Muslim community. He should be able to go where there are no Muslims and establish a new Muslim community. So in our religion the responsibility for guaranteeing the life of that religion and advancing the causes of that religion are on the individual as well as on the community. And in the final end, the life of the religious community depends on the life of that religion in the individual. Because once it dies in the individual, there's no hope for the community.

"TAQWAH" – FEAR, REVERENCE, AND A LOVE FOR GOD

RI: So, the foundation of our religion is faith.

WDM: Yes, it is faith. But let me explain, for something has to be explained here. The foundation of religion is faith, but that faith is "taqwah" which represents the foundation for us. And taqwah, as you know, is an Arabic Qur'anic term. It means or is translated "God fearing or God consciousness," and it's translated in many ways. But taqwah really means "regardfulness"; it is a sacred respect and a deep respect for things of deep and of great, great value. God tells us to have that regard for Him first of all, but also to have that regard even for our mothers. Let me repeat, we must have that regard even for our mothers. We are to have that regard for the precious ideas and the precious constructions in society. We have to have a sacred regard for those things that life must be supported by.

First of all it is God, but we also must have that same sacred regard for the daily things that life must be supported by. So taqwah is the beginning of the faith. To believe that there's a Greater Force, that there's a Greater One that you have to answer to, and to have fear but at the same time a love for that One – a love that makes you want to do and act to please that One. God says also to have a sacred regard for the wombs that bore you. Some translators say have a sacred regard for family relationships. You know, mother is the first one in that relationship. So taqwah is a little bit more than faith. It's faith alright, but it's something that's natural to man. Fear is natural, and reverence is also natural.

RI: Imam, would you say the important role of discipline in an Islamic life is a part of faith?

WDM: Without discipline you don't have an Islamic life. Our religion stresses faith but right along with faith it expresses deeds or actions. And it gives us a clear, plain, simple prescription for our life. So, can you have no discipline and follow the prescription that you get from the doctor? You'd be dead maybe. Well, we believe that of our religion. God has given us the Qur'an — our Holy Book. It's a prescription for our life. And we have to be disciplined people to follow it and stay out of trouble.

IMH: And that's what religion for Al-Islam means – submission. The very word means submission.

WDM: Yes, the very word, itself, implies discipline, because it means willing, peaceful surrender to God. That's the religion of Al-Islam. The one who believes in that is called a Muslim, and "Muslim" means one who has resigned himself to that discipline. And our greeting is "As-Salaamu-Alaikum."

RI: And our return is "Wa-Alaikum As-Salaam."

WDM: Yes. It means we wish the same peaceful life for you – for my brothers and sisters and for all people really.

RI: I've read that the greeting in itself is a prayer. That when you give a person peace you're wishing them the perfect peace that only God can give them.

WDM: Certainly it is, because the term, "The Peace," is also a name of God for Muslims. We say "As-Salaamu-Alaikum," and it means the peace. We can say "Salaamu-Alaikum," but when we say "As-Salaamu-Alaikum," it means "the peace" be on you. They translate it sometimes as peace to you — that's good too, but "the peace be on you" means that you're obligated to keep the peace.

AL-ISLAM AND CHRISTIANITY
SEEN WITH A PURE HEART

RI: So, the Muslim is the peacemaker.

WDM: He should be a peacemaker. A Muslim should be a lover of peace and a peacemaker. Yes indeed!

RI: And then in the Bible it says that the children of God are peacemakers – is that right?

WDM: Certainly.

RI: So they were describing the Muslims, weren't they?

IMH: The Prophet preached the gospel of peace.

WDM: Well, now — that's too much for this segment I think, but there are so many striking resemblances between the two religions – Christianity and Al-Islam, although on the surface they may seem to be far apart. When you look at the spirit of the two religions with a pure eye, for you see, some people can't see because they're looking for something else. They're looking for something that's in their own heart. If they come innocent and look at what Allah says to us in our Holy Book, and then they look at what the Gospel says, they'll find a common spirit, a common purity, and a common hope.

THE HONORABLE DR. MARTIN LUTHER KING

RI: Imam, to change the subject a little, today is the 19th and is the celebration for Dr. Martin Luther King. What are your views about the celebration of Dr. Martin Luther King?

WDM: He's definitely a man deserving of this kind of commemoration, this kind of yearly observance. We have to be proud of America for being able to live through the conflicts and to recognize him and give him this day. And we have to also understand that though people differed with his philosophy, most of us — Muslims and non-Muslims — admire him. We are sharing the same spirit of respect for him, and we support a day of observance for him. But I'll tell you personally, I differed with his philosophy as a follower of my father, the late leader Elijah Muhammad. And now I, myself, am in the position of leadership, and I read the Book with a great amount of freedom and a really greater amount of independence from what the Honorable Elijah Muhammd taught when he was claiming or saying that he was a messenger of God. And still I find that I really can't, myself, accept Dr. King's philosophy as my philosopy, but I do admire him for it.

I believe that there are people with different philosophies and sometimes conflicting philosophies, and they all have to exist, and they all have a purpose in this world. They all make their point and make progress for man. But for myself, I believe that passive resistance and insisting upon integration is not the way. Insisting upon social justice is one thing; insisting upon integration of races is another thing. For me, I can't buy it all.

RI: So you believe in the social progress but not necessarily the forced integration.

WDM: I believe in the motive. I believe in the spirit. I respect his spirit. I know the motive was moral and excellent – that was the motive. But the methodology and the philosophy I don't accept fully.

AL-ISLAM WORKING FOR CHANGE IN SOUTH AFRICA ALSO

RI: Yes sir. Thank you. Imam, would you give us your views on the current situation in South Africa? I know we have a lot of Muslims in South Africa, and I know that there's some developments going on in South Africa with Muslims helping in trying to come from the apartheid situation that's in there.

WDM: Like Christianity has a commitment to aid the weak, the oppressed, the ignorant, the people deprived of culture and civilization, then it is the same for our religioin. We have that same commitment. But, you know, when you look at what happened historically to liberate oppressed societies or backward societies, we don't see so much religion out front. It is only in the case of Prophet Muhammad and a few others, peace be upon the Prophet.

RI: That's right.

WDM: You don't see religion out front. And I think it's the same for our religion. Unless it's a prophet, we won't see religion so much out front in it. But quietly religion is making its contribution – religion is accepting its responsibility. I know for a fact that Muslims in South Africa are very much aware of the problems of apartheid, and they have not recently started, but for a long time they have been trying to do their best to make some healthy contribution to the betterment of the situation there. One Imam about 20 years or so ago was imprisoned for his involvement, and he was killed while he was in prison. Some people think that it was the law that killed him, the police there in South Africa. We don't know for sure; I don't know for sure whether his death was an accident or not. But I know Muslims are involved and they are making contributions to a solution for the South African situation.

CHANGE MUST COME IN SOUTH AFRICA

RI: Do you feel that the situation in South Africa will change in the near future, or do you feel that the world opinion is going to have to put more pressure to bear on that situation?

WDM: No, it has to change. It was Dr. King who said this, and I'm not quoting him exactly but this is the idea that once the mind has been awakened, then there's no way to go but to freedom. So the South African Blacks' minds have been awaken to their own human value, to their equal value with every other man, and to their responsibility to establish themselves as responsible people for their life and for their future. So they want to have their destiny in their own hands. Nothing can stop that! When it will come, we don't know. But nothing can kill it; it won't die – it's there to stay.

THE GREATEST REALIZATION OF OUR POTENTIAL IS IN SERVING ALLAH

RI: That brings me back to the question I asked you earlier about how the religion of Al-Islam awakens the importance of the role of the individual, the value of his life, and gives him a substance.

WDM: Well, first of all, the religion of Al-Islam makes every believer see that he is in the employment of God. You hear Christian preachers, as I have heard Christian preachers give text like that, that "I'm in the employment of God." Well, our religion says that you all are the Ibad of God, meaning that you are servants; you're serving God. In our religion there's no priesthood; you don't go through the priest. You go directly to God. Every man, woman, and child even is to know that he's supposed to go directly to God. So we have direct access to God; we commune with Him directly, and we're told that we're responsible to Him directly. That He has assigned to us a job. We have a job, for we are in His employment. And that job starts with the smallest responsibility that you can give a human being, and it goes up to the highest responsibility you can give a human being. How much more important can you make an individual than what is done in his religion?

IMH: You know the way you bring that out to explain the success of an individual, it stops the individual from feeling that he has to be in some big gang or something like that. There's so much he can do as an individual.

WDM: Yes. Whether it's a gang situation or working for General Motors and saying, "I'm going to rise up - I'm going to rise up in this company. One day I'm going to be president." No matter what kind of a social situation it is for the individual the individual, is naturally looking for an opportunity to get some kind of recognition to himself for his own qualifications and for his own possibilities.

What greater hope is there for the realization of our own potential than serving God, if you believe there is a God that made everything? It is God Who is responsible for the existence of everything; He's responsible for the design in the creation and responsible for even the potential in me. So what greater hope is there for me to realize this potential than by serving God? If you serve God, it's unlimited. If I serve you or the president of General Motors, it's limited. So we should seek to realize our potential and to perform the excellence that we are able to perform within society and through society by the means available to us in society, but don't have society as the last hope for that. No, God is the hope for that, and God should be the aim in our life - to please Him, to meet the demands that He has placed on us. And that means endless growth for me; there's no limit on how much I can grow. And that's how come America is so great, because many of the Founding Fathers were inspired with that kind of idea.

IMH: Is there any neutral ground for an individual, then?

WDM: Neutral ground?

IMH: Yes.

WDM: I don't think so. If you mean to be out of it, no. If you're out of it, you're not going to have anything. You either have to be in or you don't get anything. You might get something for a while, but in the end you lose everything.

MOTHERS MUST DEVELOP THE NEW SOCIETAL LIFE!

RI: Imam, is there anymore to say on the role of motherhood in society?

WDM: Yes. We believe the role of motherhood is to protect the cradle of life. The cradle of life is the little children, the home life, the disciplines that should be in an intelligent civilization and society – to see that those disciplines are imparted to her children; to support excellence in society and instill that kind of sensitivity into her children; to come to the aid of not only her husband, but to come to the aid of the public and of the government. If she sees that life is in serious danger she is to come out and express herself and demand recognition to the problem. We see that as the main role for women, and that's where their main value lies. But you know as one Jewish woman told me on a program, "Well, what about when she's through with raising children? She has nothing? She retires from that and has nothing?" No, she still has something, if she wants to continue to work for the betterment of homes and children. She doesn't have to have children; she can work for other people. But beyond that she can even feel comfortable being a doctor, being a lawyer, going into science and industry. There's nothing in our religion that says women shouldn't go into those areas of life or activity. But they say, "Well, can she be an Imam?" And I say, "No." I say "Can she be a priest in the Catholic church?" They say, "Not yet."

THE MAN IN AL-ISLAM STRIVES FOR EXCELLENE

RI: Yes sir. Brother Imam, is there anymore to say on the role of man in society, the father?

WDM: Yes. The role of man in the society is to carry the precious life that God intended for the home, to see that the precious life is protected in the public. The main role for man is to secure the public life. God has given him the physiology over the many thousands of years of history, and God has also given him this experience because of his physiology to deal with problems of the field and of public life. So the main role of man is to secure the blessings of society that God has made possible for us. That's the main role for man. But all men can't do that. That's for a few men. All men can support that, but all men can't be involved. Government people have few people dedicated in certain restricted fields of knowledge. So where is the role for *all* men then? The role for all men is to work in their respective places, but to know that their job should also compliment the big picture. Their job should be supportive of the greatest aims of society.

So, though we're happy, for I was happy as a welder. I think I could be happy as a welder again, if I had to. I could be happy as a welder, because I don't have to be conscious of this great role that God has for the top man in civilization or in society. But I have this urge to perform excellence; that my work comes out the best and that my welding work comes out to be the best. Being motivated toward excellence in my life I serve a role or I'm acting out that role. Any person that wants excellence in his life and insists upon excellent performance in his own life, he's already in that big role. So I think I can reduce it down to that much. That if we just strive for excellence, strive to be our best and don't be satisfied with sloppy performance, don't be satisfied with vulgarity and stupidity, then you'll be acting in that big role.

THE AMERICAN SOCIETY SHOULD RESEARCH AL-ISLAM

RI: Imam, do you feel that if the American society could get an honest look at Al-Islam that they would begin to see the great benefit and the role that Al-Islam has played in world history?

WDM: Allah God says in our Book to those who feel that this is some kind of a threat to their society, God says why don't they do a research of this Book? Any intelligent person who does an honest research of our Holy Book will say, "Well, maybe I don't think I want to put myself through that. I'm going to stay with Budddhism. I'm going to stay with the Gospel. I'll stay with the Torah, the law of Moses." They may say that. But they won't say that "I can't live with this next door to me." I've had Christians who really got the wrong image of Muslims tell me on the radio, "Well Mister, now that I understand what that religion is, if everybody would practice as you're doing, I'd be happy to have you as my neighbor."

RI: Well, Imam. We have certainly enjoyed you being here. And as I said once before, the door is alway open for you.

WDM: Thank you. I feel very comfortable here in Pittsburgh. If it wasn't so cold, and if it was a little warmer than Chicago, I'd move here.

RI: We don't have any control over the weather but. . .

WDM: I know.

RI: So thank you very much for coming here and giving us the opportunity to express our Islamic views and get greater insight on our Islamic religion. I know Imam Hassain would like to also give his appreciation for you coming here today.

IMH: Yes sir, always.

WDM: Well, thank you. I've been your guest many times, and always I've felt that I benefit personally when I'm around you. I've admired you for a long time.

IMH: Well, the way I feel about Imam Muhammad is that when he comes, he comes like a person handing you tools to work with. And the statement now is when you get tools, you have to start using them.

RI: Yes sir. Well, we have to close out. We thank you for being here and we thank the public for watching our program, "Al-Islam in Focus." We hope that we've given you some benefit. We give you the greetings in the Qur'an and Arabic language "As-Salaamu-Alaikum."

WDM
   &   Wa-Alaikum As-Salaam.
IMH

HELP THE MUSLIM AMERICAN COMMUNITY ASSISTANCE FUND

W. Deen Mohammed authors many publications and makes many personal appearances throughout the United States in an effort to spread the truth of Al-Islam as taught by the Holy Qur'an. Persons who desire to support his efforts are asked to send their contributions to the following address:

W. Deen Mohammed Propagation
M.A.C.A. Fund
P. O. Box 1061
Calumet City, Illinois 60409
Please make donations payable to: M.A.C.A Fund

----------------------------Cut along this line------------------------

Please find enclosed for the W. Deen Mohammed Propagation M.A.C.A. Fund a donation in the amount of:

[ ]$50.00 [ ]$25.00 [ ]$15.00 [ ]$10.00 [ ]$5.00

[ ] _____Other

Donor Information:

Name:_____

Address:_____ Apt:_____

City:_____ State:_____ Zip:_____

THANK YOU!

NOTE: Donor information is necessary in order that a receipt is returned for donations received.